FATHERHOOD

THE MISSING LINK

D1568458

FATHERHOOD
THE MISSING LINK

RESTORING GOD'S ORDER FOR FAMILY

JOHN EDMONDSON

VICTORY IN CHRIST CHRISTIAN CENTER
WESTVILLE, NJ

Fatherhood: The Missing Link
Copyright © 2017 by John Edmonson
ISBN 13: 978-1-5323-4575-3

Published by *Victory in Christ Christian Center*
1055 Delsea Drive
Westville, NJ 08093

Visit our website at victoryinchrist.cc

Printed in the United States of America

This book is dedicated to the people without whom I would not be the man, husband and father I am today:

My heartfelt thanks to Bishop I.V. and Pastor Bridget Hilliard, my spiritual father and mother, for your constant example of Fatherhood and Motherhood that constantly inspires me to keep growing and walking by faith. I can never repay you for all that you have done and continue to do for me personally and our church overall.

I am forever grateful to the late Dr. Lamont McLean, who was a father in the faith, and the late Dr. Myles Munroe, a spiritual mentor. These two men were used by God to drastically alter, shape and fashion the man of God I have become.

Special thanks to my mother, Patricia J. Edmondson; your strength has always been unfathomable and the confidence you instilled in me, as well as the belief that I can do anything I put my mind to do, have been the catalyst for who I am today.

To Isha, my beautiful bride, helpmeet, wife, best friend, mother of our children, co-pastor and co-laborer of all that God has called us to do. Thank you for taking this journey of faith with me. Your unconditional love, commitment and dedication form the wind beneath my wings that has truly helped me fly in life.

And most of all, to my three sons, Joshua, Christian and Jordan. You are the three main reasons I wrote this book. Outside of God, you guys are my drive and commitment to be the best father I can be. May my life and this book serve as a guide and be the progenerational foundation for you to become the fathers you are destined to be.

∽

CONTENTS

INTRODUCTION

Fatherhood matters to God. It is so important that, in the New Testament, God reveals Himself as our "Heavenly Father". Today, we see a clear crisis in fatherhood in society. In the United States, one third of all children grow up in a household without a biological father. A father's absence from the home creates a void which manifests in psychological and behavioral handicaps in the children.

According to publicly available research, when children grow up in a home without a father, they are four times more likely to live in poverty. A child without a father's guidance is more likely to commit crime and go to prison. A female child is seven times more likely to become pregnant as a teen when there is no father present. Children in homes without fathers are more likely to experience abuse and mistreatment. And, they are two times more likely to drop out of school. There is a crisis in fatherhood that affects our children.

Most of the issues and ills of society can be traced to the absence or inactivity of a father. It's time for this trend to stop. But, it can only be reversed when men allow God to father them and then be the father that God designed for them to be. It is not easy being a father—it takes more than providing the seed for pregnancy. Fatherhood occurs before a man even enters into marriage and continues through the life of a child. Fatherhood is not produced in a one night stand but through a deliberate process of fathering.

That's why I wrote this book. I come from a home where my biological father and my step-father walked out on us. Because of my mother's love and determination and God's intervention, I did not continue the negative patterns of manhood and fatherhood that I had experienced. And, I didn't become a negative statistic.

Now, as I see my three sons become men in their own right, I have a passion to teach other men how to submit to the fathering process so that they can become fathers who please God and bless their families.

In this book, I explain the process that God took me through to understand what it means to be a father and not just a man. God has expectations for a man who walks in fatherhood and I clearly define those roles and responsibilities. My prayer is that whether you are a single man, a married man, a wife or a single woman, you would embrace and honor the unique role of fatherhood and champion it in your life, church and community.

CHAPTER 1

Restoring FATHERHOOD

Restoring
FATHERHOOD

This is no ordinary book! The truth that this book contains will change lives—both yours and your family's. If your family has experienced struggle after struggle and just can't seem to move forward, this book will give you the information you've desperately sought. There is a piece of the puzzle that has been overlooked and its absence has prevented God's full picture from emerging. When a cake is baked without all the necessary ingredients, it may look like a cake on the outside but once you eat it you know something is missing. This is the current state of the family! It has lost certain ingredients, which prevents it from tasting good. This book restores the proper recipe to the family by firmly establishing the role and ministry of the father.

For men, when you read this book, you will gain a greater understanding of your identity and your God-given fatherhood role. For single women, this book sets the standard for what a man should be so that in the dating process you will know what to look for. This book challenges all that you thought you knew. Misperceptions will be corrected. Areas where you lacked understanding will be filled. This is going to be a very life-changing journey.

I must state honestly that this book will make some readers angry! I wrestled with this as I wrote; however, there has been too much silence about the topic of fatherhood, and our families and men are suffering. Others will be enlightened by Biblical truths of which you were unaware. I believe you will have many revelatory moments as you read this book. Feel free to take notes in the margins. Don't just read it like a novel but engage with it like a manual so that the book's principles become a part of your life. I believe that **Fatherhood: The Missing Link** will complete whatever ingredients are missing from your life and family regardless of how elusive and difficult they may have seemed in the past.

If you grew up without a father, this book is for you. If your father was in the home but wasn't there, this book is for you. If you're married and your family is not where it needs to be, this book is for you. If you're a single male or female and you believe you're supposed to be married, then most certainly this book is for you.

Before we go any further, let me warn you. The continual reading of this book on fatherhood will result in dramatic changes in your life and the lives of those connected to you. If you are tired of the mundane and ready for a true, life-altering experience, keep reading. If you are not ready for that kind of change, put this book down and go no further until you are really ready to become everything God destined for you to be. My prayer is that every person who reads this book will experience life on a higher level.

> *"They know not, neither will they understand;*
> *they walk on in darkness:*
> *all the foundations of the earth are out of course.*
> *I have said, Ye are gods;*
> *and all of you are children of the most High."*

PSALM 82:5-6, KJV

God chastises His people because even though they are considered gods and children of the most High, they have gotten off course and walk in darkness. This is the current state of fatherhood and the family. We are supposed to have blessed and happy homes but our families struggle consistently. The absence of the fatherhood ministry is due to three causes. First is a *lack of knowledge*. If you don't know something, you are headed for trouble. The Bible says, ***"My people are destroyed for lack of knowledge"*** **(Hosea 4:6, KJV).** The second thing that will cause problems in your life (and this is really in *any* area of your life) is a *lack of comprehension*. The third is *walking in ignorance*—knowing that you do not know something but doing nothing to gain knowledge. That's what Psalm 82:5 addresses. If you don't understand something, you are headed for trouble. If you lack knowledge, you're headed for trouble. If you don't understand something, you're headed for trouble. All three of these—lack of knowledge, lack of comprehension and walking in ignorance—always create problems in your life.

Have you ever noticed the frustration level of someone who doesn't understand a concept? I recall times when I tried to assemble something and became frustrated because I just could not understand the instructions—or the lack of instructions. Few things are more frustrating than not knowing how something works. God does not like ignorance. Why? Because at the root of ignorance is the word *ignore*. God does not like ignorance because, at its core, it means that someone ignored something important. The more you ignore a problem, the worse it gets. If you're ignorant about something, it's a reflection of your failure to spend time with God. I say that because if you spend time with God, He will reveal to you everything you need to know. If you walk around in frustration long enough, failure is a relief. My hope is that you will get to a point where you are not ignorant so that you won't be frustrated any longer.

"Wisdom is the principal thing;
therefore, get wisdom: and with all thy getting
get understanding."

PROVERBS 4:7, KJV

The Bible says that wisdom is the principal thing. Especially with respect to the things of God, you must put yourself in a position to get as much wisdom as possible. If you intentionally put yourself in an atmosphere where God's principles are being taught, you will receive wisdom for living. This may happen in a conference, church service or book. To gain wisdom, you must make time available because wisdom is the principal thing. Look at how the Amplified Bible says it.

"The beginning of Wisdom is: get Wisdom
(skillful and godly Wisdom)!
[For skillful and godly Wisdom is the principal thing.]
And with all you have gotten, get understanding
(discernment, comprehension, and interpretation)."

PROVERBS 4:7, AMP

One of the weaknesses I see in people who attend church regularly is that they catch the emotion of church but miss the principles. They "have church" but miss getting "an understanding." We jump really well and shout really well and all those things, but we don't get an understanding. What good is the Word if you don't have understanding?

"If any of you lack wisdom, let him ask of God,
that giveth to all men liberally, and upbraideth not;
and it shall be given him."

JAMES 1:5, KJV

Look at how the Amplified version states it.

"If any of you is deficient in wisdom, let him ask of the giving God [Who gives] to everyone liberally and ungrudgingly, without reproaching or faultfinding, and it will be given him."

JAMES 1:5, AMP

In other words, if you ask God for wisdom, He will give it to you even if you don't deserve it. Even if you made mistakes as recently as this week or even today, or you made God a promise and didn't follow through, if you say to God, "God, I need wisdom," He will give it to you. That should be exciting to you because it means that on your job, if you don't know how to complete a project that's been assigned to you, all you have to do (if you're a Christian) is ask God for wisdom and God will give it to you—and give it to you liberally.

God is so committed to getting wisdom to you that He will not even allow your lack of a prayer life to disqualify you. "Why," you may ask? It's very simple: God knows that you cannot make it without wisdom. If my child struggles in mathematics and I didn't do well in math, God will give me the wisdom to either help them or get them to the right person who can help them. If my marriage is struggling, when I ask God for wisdom, He'll tell me what to do. God will tell me what to say to my spouse. Sometimes we don't know what to say to them. I know there are men reading this who would attest to that. Sometimes we don't know what to say to our wives. She says something and I'm at a loss. Your wife may ask, "Why did you do that, honey?" And you respond, "I have no idea." Your wife will then say, "Didn't I tell you?" "Yes, you did." There are times when we cause problems in our own homes and need God's wisdom to get it straight. I am so thankful to God that every time I have asked Him for wisdom concerning my marriage, family, ministry or life, He has never failed me—and He won't fail you, either.

If you need wisdom, God will give it to you. I remember as a child watching my mother, a single mom, stretch $10 over two weeks' time and feed three hungry boys in the process. I never understood how she could do this until I grew older and realized that God was helping her determine how to spend her limited resources. It is the same with this principle of fatherhood! If you don't know the principles of fatherhood, you'll never be able to walk as a true Biblical father. There are principles, or formulas, to fatherhood. It is very similar to those who know mathematics. Once you learn the formulas, you are able to solve any problem.

It's the same with fatherhood. There is a pattern. There is a formula. There are principles, and no matter what the situation, if you know the formula, you can resolve the problem. Many of us are trying to make fatherhood fit the way we know how to do it—or the way we were taught. We are operating from what we saw our fathers do (or from what our fathers failed to do). We're trying to father the best way we know how but our way is not the best way. The best way is to operate our lives exactly the way God purposed them to be. Let's look at the purpose of a male man.

"And when Abram was ninety years old and nine,
the Lord appeared to Abram, and said unto him,
I am the Almighty God; walk before me, and be thou perfect. And I
will make my covenant between me and thee, and
will multiply thee exceedingly."

GENESIS 17:1, KJV

Now, let's stop for a second. I want you to get this. The average man today does not know who he is. Abraham didn't know at this point who he was, nor did he know where he was supposed to go. This is key: *If a man doesn't know who he is, he will not know where he is going.* So, if you are in a relationship with a man who does not know who he is, he will not be able to lead your family. It's a case of the blind leading the blind.

When Abraham was around 90 years old, God appeared to him to give him clarity about who he was and where his life was supposed to go. There will be a lot of men sneaking into heaven, but they're going to have to stand before God and answer to Him because they never found out who they were and where they were supposed to be going. It is a shame to see a man wandering through life not knowing who he is.

Some men try to gain material things. Materialism does not define you and will never truly satisfy you. In the same fashion, a lack of materialism does not define you either. In professional sports, some players are making millions of dollars but are not satisfied. They have a summer home, a winter home, a fall home, a spring home. They have yachts, they have clothes, they have cars and still they contemplate suicide because while they possess everything the world is chasing, they're neither truly happy nor satisfied. Please remember this: Money and things will never truly satisfy you. You may say, "Well, I sure would like to give it a whirl and see how it makes me feel." As logical as that may sound, the reality is, you're not built to be satisfied by money and materialism, but rather by discovering and walking in your God-ordained purpose.

When God appeared to Abram, here is what happened: "...**Abram fell on his face: and God talked with him…**" (Genesis 17:3). Men, if you really want to find out who you are, you must get on your face before God. God will not talk to you if you do not put your face before Him. Let me tell you why. When a man puts his face down before God, it is an act of humility. Many men struggle with the process of getting before the Lord. Women, on the other hand, can easily get before God. In a worship service, women can praise God from their core while tears flow down their cheeks, causing their makeup to run down their faces. For most men, it's not that easy because we're dealing with our pride. For a man to lift his hands and truly worship, he must be truly mature in the Lord or be having an encounter with The Holy Ghost at that moment.

Brother, if you are to be everything God wants you to be, God requires that you change your perception of worship. Worship participation is not a feminine trait or behavior. It is the first calling of a man! We, as men, must learn to fall on our faces before God. If you want God to talk to you, put your face in front of God before you pick up the daily news. God did not talk to Abram until he fell on his face. Then God said, *"As for me, behold, my covenant is with thee, and thou shalt be a father of many nations…"* (Genesis 17:4). When God made a covenant with Abram, he called forth destiny in him: *"…I will make you a father"* (Genesis17:4). Why would this be the first thing God said to Abram? It's because every boy has fatherhood potential inside of him. If every boy has this potential, it must mean that every boy is supposed to step into fatherhood, though not every boy does.

What is a father? The Hebrew word for father is *Ab*. The Greek word for father is the *Pater*. The word *Abba* (Aramaic) means "source that takes responsibility." Fertilizing an egg does not make a man a father. It makes you a male but not a father. That's the difference between a male and a father. Males can inseminate females. However, a father starts, maintains, protects, upholds, nourishes, provides for and sustains his children.

God is a prime example of the fatherhood ministry.

"Who being the brightness of his glory, and the express image of his person, and upholding all things by the word of his power, when he had by himself purged our sins, sat down on the right hand of the Majesty on high…"

HEBREWS 1:3

God always upholds anyone connected to Him. This is important because if you are one of God's children, he must uphold you. Even if you don't feel upheld, he must uphold you. God not only upholds all those associated with Him, He also takes responsibility for all His children. God watches over His children.

People may have counted you out and even worked against you; nevertheless, you made it. Why do you think this happened? Because your good Father was working on your behalf! This is very personal to me because I had people tell me, "You'll never amount to anything. You'll never make it. You're just like your daddy." They were right, but they had the wrong person. I'm just like my daddy, but you got me mixed up with the wrong Daddy.

I'm just like my spiritual Daddy, even though my natural daddy walked out of my life at the age of two and my stepfather walked away from my life at the age of 12. God said, "That's fine because I really don't need you specifically to get the job done. I'll get to him myself through others whom I will send into his life to be fatherhood." God made a vow. He said, *"I'll be a father to the fatherless"* (Psalm 68:5). So, the minute a natural father says, "I don't want to accept my responsibility of fatherhood," God says, "Fine. I'll step in and do the job the way it was supposed to be done." A father takes responsibility for anyone he produces. I want to show you another name for father.

"This is the book of the generations of Adam.
In the day that God created man,
in the likeness of God made he him."

GENESIS 5:1

That word *created* is *Bara* in Hebrew. It means to bring forth from nothing. In other words, "In the day that God brought forth man from nothing." Then it says, *"...in the likeness of God made he him..."* "Made" is the word *Asah* in Hebrew, which means "to restore." God is bringing out a principle that He produces something from nothing and then restores it. God establishes a pattern of how the male man should operate within his home. Keep reading, it's about to get a little rough. Remember, the Bible says *"And ye shall know the truth, and the truth shall make you free" (John 8:32).* Sometimes the process of freedom is painful because you must dislodge those things that have become attached to you; but once you are free, it feels so good.

You have seen me use the term "male man" and I want to take a moment to explain why.

"Male and female created he them; and blessed them, and called their name Adam, in the day when they were created."

GENESIS 5:2

Adam in Hebrew means "man." So, according to Scripture, God made a male man and a female man and blessed them. Even though they are two separate beings, they were created to function together. This is why it is so important for a male man to know his purpose and position—so that he can fulfill his part of God's plan for the family. Let me show you this in Scripture. You will recall that God made male and female in His image.

"And God said, Let us make man in our image, after our likeness: and let them have dominion over the fish of the sea, and over the fowl of the air, and over the cattle, and over all the earth, and over every creeping thing that creepeth upon the earth. So God created man in his own image, in the image of God created he him; male and female created he them. And God blessed them, and God said unto them, Be fruitful, and multiply, and replenish the earth, and subdue it: and have dominion over the fish of the sea, and over the fowl of the air, and over every living thing that moveth upon the earth."

GENESIS 1:26-28

God blessed the male and female man and told both of them to have dominion! When God established the family, he expected that family to operate in the same manner He does. God created us in His image, and when a male man has a wife and family, he produces after his own kind. Here is an example:

"And Adam lived a hundred and thirty years, and begat a son in his own likeness, after his image; and called his name Seth."

GENESIS 5:3

Adam followed God's pattern. He produced offspring in his own image and then gave that child a name. This is an important concept that demonstrates the power that God has placed in the male man's hands. When you—as a married man—have a child, you are fulfilling a pattern that God established. You produce a life and then you speak destiny and purpose into that life.

Another name for "father" is "beginning of ancestry." If you were to look up the word *father*, you would find that one of the definitions is "beginning of ancestry" because the father is the one who gives identity to what he produces. In other words, your son or daughter might come from you and look like you in your image or in your likeness, but you must bring them to where they reflect you. A father not only produces something after himself, he also hangs around long enough for the thing he produces to reflect him. In other words, the fatherhood role is fulfilled not at the point of birth but through the life of those children until they reflect the image of their father. This requires an investment of time on the part of the man. Often, mothers are left to rear the children while the father simply provides. This is an imbalanced and incomplete role of the father and it contradicts the fatherhood model of God. As men, we must move beyond celebrating the fact that our sons look like us. The real issue is whether or not they live like men of God as they grow and mature. This is a serious and solemn responsibility that God has given the man!

When a man marries a woman, she becomes his responsibility. Her father was responsible for her until he walked her down to the altar. When he turned her over to her husband, the responsibility of the father ended and the husband's responsibility as father, source and covering began.

The Bible says, *"Therefore shall a man leave his father and his mother, and shall cleave unto his wife: and they shall be one flesh" (Genesis 2:24).* That woman should now be able to cleave to the fatherhood covering and protection that she has most likely known all her life.

This is vital. If you are dating a man who lacks an understanding of his God-given purpose and direction, do not marry him until he has clearly understood the fatherhood ministry that God intends for him to fulfill. It will save you a lot of misery in the future. His ignorance of his role as fatherhood in your life may cause you unnecessary heartache and pain and leave a continual open door for the enemy to attack you and everything you hold dear. Regardless of how much you are attracted to a man, regardless of how much you love him, you must love yourself more and not settle for less than what God has destined for your life. You must let him know "I love you, but I can't marry you right now because you don't know who you truly are and what you are called to be. Therefore, you don't know who I am and the responsibility you will have in helping me become who God has called me to be."

At the heart of this book is a heart for people and married couples. What really hits me at the core is seeing couples struggle when they don't have to. I don't like seeing a man who won't lead his family. God has convicted me to help our men get in their place. My wife and I are certified Christian counselors and we really have a heart for couples; we want couples to be blessed. Any time we have done premarital counseling, we tell couples, "We really don't care about your wedding day. We love you and we're going to celebrate with you, but we're not after your wedding day. We're preparing you for 10 years into your marriage, 15 years into your marriage, 20 years into your marriage." We want your marriage to be awesome long after your wedding day has come and gone. Too many people invest more time getting ready for their wedding day than for the lifelong commitment of marriage to this other person. The Bible talks many times about the commitment of marriage.

"Husbands, love your wives, even as Christ also loved the church, and gave himself for it; that he might sanctify and cleanse it with the washing of water by the word, that he might present it to himself a glorious church, not having spot, or wrinkle, or any such thing; but that it should be holy and without blemish. So ought men to love their wives as their own bodies. He that loveth his wife loveth himself."

EPHESIANS 5:25

This is just one example of the commitment level that should be in your marriage. Men, if you treat yourself well, you should treat your wife well. For all the single women reading this right now who are in a relationship and wondering if he is the one, assess the man based on what you learn in this book and make a wise decision. The man should value you as much as he values himself.

"For no man ever yet hated his own flesh; but nourisheth and cherisheth it, even as the Lord the church"

EPHESIANS 5:29

The husband is to cherish, nourish and protect his wife.

This means that women must change their approach to relationships. Your criteria for a man must go beyond his financial position and his physical attributes. You should assess a man based on his relationship with God and his understanding of his role toward you. Does he value you by opening the door? Does he verbally express your worth? Does he acknowledge your beauty? Some men don't do this naturally because they did not have a father in their lives. Some women don't even know to expect these things because they never saw it done in their homes.

A male will simply deposit seed to produce a child. A male man will fulfill his fatherhood ministry by representing God and seeking God's purpose for everyone in the home. The fatherhood role protects, provides and pushes everyone around him.

The fatherhood ministry is committed to a process of development that takes people from the beginning to a successful conclusion (maturity). A male man will see that his role doesn't end when a child is born. The job is just beginning at that point. Fatherhood finishes what he started. Whether you meant to start it or not, whether it surprised you or not, fatherhood finishes.

You see examples all around of how the idea of fatherhood has become perverted. In our society, we need the government to track down a man to support his child. This shows that the world doesn't understand fatherhood. A father should not have to be tracked down! He will hang around and make sure the thing he produces conforms to him. This is true biblical fatherhood: taking the next generation from infancy to spiritual destiny and maturity.

What happens in the life of the father affects the entire family. There is actually research that shows that if the father follows God, the rest of the family will follow. It is not God's intended design for women to be the spiritual leaders in the home. God's model is never that the mother and children go to church and the father goes to the golf course. A father is a spiritual model.

A father is also a creator. I want to show you something in the Scripture about the male man as creator in his family.

"In the beginning was the Word, and the Word was with God, and the Word was God. The same was in the beginning with God. All things were made by him; and without him was not any thing made that was made."

....

JOHN 1:1

....

Scripture testifies that God, through the Word, created all things. God is a creator and so is the father. A father is more than a creator of children. He creates opportunities and solves problems. So, when a father comes home and everyone starts to say, "Daddy, Daddy, Daddy," it should never be seen as a nuisance. It is a time when those children are calling on the creative potential within him. When they present issues, concerns or situations, it is not to pile on but to draw out what God has put within the male man. This fatherhood ministry includes his wife.

Sadly, in some homes, the wife/mother is left to handle the finances and all the problems for the family while the man stands idly by. This is out of order and I call on women to release themselves from that solo burden. Even if the wife is the better person with finances, it should be done with the support and input of the husband/father. God strategically positioned the male man to be in the home to represent God. His input enhances situations and should never detract or worsen them. This means that male men make the time to be fully engaged in their families' lives. A male man should never be present-yet-absent! In our culture, women are encouraged to be both the mother and the father. This is out of the will of God! The woman should be the mother and give room for the man to be who God positioned him to be.

The point I am trying to make is this: Women, you need to get out of the way. Move aside. Let him be a man. If he doesn't know how, let God teach him. You get out of the way. I know he is a hard worker, but he is supposed to be and then he is supposed to come home and take care of you—not the other way around—because he's a father. I can't tell you how many wives say to me in counseling, "Pastor, I wish he would just lead." The real question I ask is, "Are you willing to get out of the way?" Ladies, I know you can be independent and do things for yourselves, but he needs you to get out of the way and let him lead. Get out of the way. If you're about to get in the car and he won't open the car door, stand out there until he leads. If he is sitting in the car saying, "Come on, honey. Let's go," respond with, "I'm waiting for you to lead." He may say, "Well, I'm in the car already." "No, no, no. My male man would open my door for me."

When the two of you travel together, allow him to lead by sitting in the car and waiting for him to open your door for you. It may initially cause tension and even frustration but this type of action is necessary to call forth the male man within your husband. If your husband bristles at you, remind him that God has created him to protect, nourish, cherish and take care of you.

Until this level of fatherhood is clearly understood, a man should never contemplate marriage, let alone procreate. If there's any man reading this whose wife is leading, that is a sign that you don't have ownership. A man who has ownership and knows he's a father will not let anybody lead except him. Every man was created, fashioned and formed to be a father regardless of his upbringing. In my own life, I had two fathers—a biological father and a stepfather. Both of them walked away. When they walked away, I was angry and I was upset and I was mad. I wanted nothing to do with them. God kept pressing me about where my heart was on the matter. I had so many questions. "Why did they leave? Why don't they want to be around me? What's wrong with me? It's my fault." All this nonsense, over and over and over again. I walked around angry and with a chip on my shoulder, and God dealt with me once I went into the ministry. "You're not effective for me because every problem is a fatherhood problem. For you to minister effectively to men, you must be free yourself. If you're in bondage, you can't lead." I had to make the commitment to forgive these two men for what they did by leaving a young boy to fend for himself in a cruel world. I had to forgive them—not because they deserved it, but so that I could be free from what they had done and step into my destiny. Forgiveness takes the pain that others inflict upon you and ultimately releases you from it and from what they did. If you are a man reading this and your father was not there for you, I am a living witness that you can overcome this terrible situation. You can rise from the ashes of this calamity and be a better man and father than the one who didn't fulfill his fatherhood responsibility in your life.

You must realize you're not the first to experience this. For many men, their father wasn't there when they were growing up. For some, their father was in the house but not in their lives because he was working all the time. I encourage you to settle once and for all the fact that your father did not fulfill his responsibilities. Resolve, eulogize and bury this painful fact so that you don't have to stay stuck in that place—the place of pain, rejection and feeling like something is wrong with you. What takes you from that harsh, rejected place to a place of freedom that breaks a cycle of repetitive behavior is extending forgiveness to your father. If you don't resolve within yourself to forgive him, there is a high probability that you will do the same thing to your family. Even if you are physically there, the emotional baggage that stays packed within you will cause emotional—and maybe even physical—fractures in the ones you love.

I have committed to myself and to God that my three sons— Joshua, Christian and Jordan—will never experience fatherlessness the way I did. I am also dedicated to helping many other men recover from the fatherlessness in their own lives. If we can heal a generation of men from the devastation of fatherlessness, we can impact the generations coming behind us. We can foster and release the spirit of fatherhood in the way God intended.

Men, we must get fatherhood right. We must get fatherhood right in our homes and in the church because without it our homes and the church will never be right. Every problem is a fatherhood problem, and the world will stay off course until fatherhood comes back. I believe we can and will assume our rightful place once again.

CHAPTER 2

Defining FATHERHOOD

A s I stated in the last chapter, I—like so many other men—grew up with a fatherhood void in my life. My biological father was there until I was two years old, and then he was gone. My stepfather was there until I was 12, and then he was gone. I can remember my stepfather saying "I love you" only one time. I remember him playing basketball with me one time. I played football all my life. In my mind, I was the greatest football player ever. My stepfather came to see me play one time. He didn't even come for the whole game. He came for one quarter. He came late and left early. Looking back at what both of the men in my life did and didn't do, I understand now that both of them couldn't be the father I needed them to be because neither one of them understood fatherhood. Here is a wisdom principle: *"You cannot be what you don't understand."* Even if you have knowledge, without understanding you will walk in darkness. Possessing knowledge of something isn't enough. If you don't have an understanding of it, you're going to walk in darkness. So many men don't understand fatherhood, so they can't walk as fathers.

Again, the word "father" means a source that nourishes, sustains, maintains, provides, protects and upholds. Fatherhood is so awesome and so important that God called Himself a father. This is a truth all men must embrace. The highest honor you can hold in the Kingdom of God is not a preacher or any of the other five-fold ministry gifts. The highest honor a man can ever hold is walking in fatherhood. God's purpose and design for the man is to be a father. Success is not money. Success is not business. Success is not even elevation in the church. Success is not a title. Success for a man is walking in true fatherhood.

Without a father in his life, a male man has no identity. If you grew up without a father like I did, and even if your father was there but didn't understand fatherhood, you should seek out a father who understands fatherhood, who is willing to take responsibility for you. There's a Scripture that says,

> *"For though ye have ten thousand instructors in Christ,*
> *yet have ye not many fathers: for in Christ Jesus*
> *I have begotten you through the gospel."*

1 CORINTHIANS 4:15

An instructor will be committed to teaching you but a father is willing to take responsibility for you. There is a big difference between teaching me and being responsible for me. Let me tell you how this affected me. When my wife and I started our church, we knew how to start a church, how to make contracts and how to establish nonprofit status. We knew how to acquire buildings. We learned from a great instructor but the instructor wasn't our Spiritual Father. He took responsibility for teaching us ministry but not responsibility for us and our destiny. As a result, I knew how to be a pastor and do ministry but I didn't know how to be a spiritual father.

Pastors who have never been fathered themselves cannot father others and can see the value of people only in terms of how they affect the ministry of which they are a part instead of the ministry they have inside themselves. I experienced frustration early in the ministry we started. I did not realize why things were not going as I had planned. Our first service, 59 people showed up but they just came to say, "Hey, we support you." Then we went down to 11. We had 11 people. We began to grow and people began coming in. We went up to 45 people and then we stopped. We hit a wall. I had no idea what was happening and why the growth did not continue.

I remember it so clearly! God said, "You need your spiritual father and can go no further on your own." I replied, "Okay, who are you telling us to go to?" God ordered our steps, and we finally were able to connect with the late Dr. Lamont and Pastor Connie Mclean. As we connected with our spiritual parents and came under fatherhood, all of a sudden growth took place. Within a week's time, things started moving. People started coming into the church. Revenue increased for us to do things we were unable to do previously. The greatest change occurred in me! Our church family began to say, "Pastor, something happened to you." They recognized that there was a new level of revelation flowing out of me. There was a different anointing. I'll never forget this one occurrence: I went to preach a men's retreat for Pastor Lamont and at the end, I began to minister to the men. After I finished that time of ministry, Dr. Lamont, my dad in the Gospel, approached me. I started crying like a baby! He embraced me and declared, "I am your father." He continued, "I break every curse. I break every negative thing that was spoken over you. I break instructors who tried to hold you down. I have the authority to do this because I am your spiritual father."

Well, I wouldn't let him go. I grabbed him tighter and wouldn't let him go because I was in my daddy's arms. He said, "I'm saying these things to you because you need to be walking in fatherhood and you need to be able to break things over your spiritual children one day." That day, I received my identity. My purpose was clear to me and I could walk in fatherhood because I was under fatherhood. I believe this book was birthed in me at that moment.

Every male man must know his identity but he can't receive it unless he hears his father's voice. This same thing happened to Jesus!

"After his baptism, as Jesus came up out of the water, the heavens were opened and he saw the Spirit of God descending like a dove and settling on him. And a voice from heaven said, "This is my dearly loved Son, who brings me great joy."

MATTHEW 3:16

This was God's voice establishing Jesus' purpose and expressing God's approval! This is what many men lack. When God speaks over your life, His spirit is able to lead you. This happened to Jesus.

"Then Jesus was led by the Spirit into the wilderness to be tempted there by the devil."

MATTHEW 4:1

Many people misunderstand that the power in that moment was not the water baptism but the voice of his Father. Many of you reading this book haven't heard your father's voice because you didn't have your father. My heartfelt prayer is that you connect into fatherhood, that you allow your father to speak into your life and tell you that you *are* a man of God. Then you *will* do what God has called you to do because you're hearing your daddy's voice. If you are feeling something tug on the inside of you right now, that is your destiny getting stirred up as it hears fatherhood calling it into manifestation.

It says that when Jesus heard his Daddy's voice, then he went. In other words, he couldn't pursue destiny until his Father said, "I'm pleased; go do it." He heard his Daddy's voice and then he said, "Now that I heard Daddy say, 'I'm pleased,' I can do what I'm called to do."

Here are some startling statistics. Eighty percent of men in prison come out of foster homes. The other 20 percent had no father in their house. One hundred percent of men who are in prison right now are the result of the inactivity or absence of a father.

"Then said Jesus to those Jews which believed on him, If ye continue in my word, then are ye my disciples indeed; And ye shall know the truth, and the truth shall make you free.

They answered him, We be Abraham's seed, and were never in bondage to any man: how sayest thou, Ye shall be made free? Jesus answered them, Verily, verily, I say unto you, Whosoever committeth sin is the servant of sin. And the servant abideth not in the house for ever: but the Son abideth ever. If the Son therefore shall make you free, ye shall be free indeed. I know that ye are Abraham's seed; but ye seek to kill me, because my word hath no place in you. I speak that which I have seen with my Father: and ye do that which ye have seen with your father. They answered and said unto him, Abraham is our father. Jesus saith unto them, If ye were Abraham's children, ye would do the works of Abraham."

JOHN 8:31-39

These are strong words from Jesus! He demonstrated to these religious leaders that they were disconnected from their true spiritual father, Abraham. The same is true today. Millions of men haven't touched their potential because they haven't been under fatherhood. As a result, they have lived out the script that their earthly fathers left them. They are walking in the same broken steps of their fathers. This book is the voice of God to you which releases you to do what you were created to do. Unfortunately, some people will resist this truth.

The Jews got mad at Jesus for teaching this revelation. The Jews said to him, "You have a problem." Jesus turned around, according to what we just read, and said, "*I* don't have a problem; *you* have a problem. You have a father problem." They said, "We don't have a father problem. Abraham was our father." Jesus said, "No, you don't even know who your father is." Why was he saying that?

*"Your father Abraham rejoiced to see my day:
and he saw it, and was glad."*

JOHN 8:56

The Jews were very angry now. They said to Jesus, "Wait a minute. You're not even 50 years old and you're saying you've seen Abraham?"

*"Jesus said unto them, Verily, verily, I say unto you,
Before Abraham was, I am."*

JOHN 8:58

Jesus corrected their misconception. They assumed that Jesus had been a contemporary of Abraham's but that was not what Jesus said. Jesus said that Abraham saw Him because Jesus was before Abraham. In fact, Jesus said, "Abraham rejoiced to see me." In other words, Jesus was saying that Abraham recognized who his Father was and walked in that blessing. However, these Jews refused to see who Abraham was in their lives and they didn't operate like Abraham did.

Abraham was excited to connect with an eternal destiny through the Son of God. This is the order of God. If you cannot get excited about the purposes and plans God has for your life, it means you are clearly disconnected from the fatherhood ministry. I pray that you will heed these words and bring your masculine self under the authority of a spiritual father who can speak destiny into you. That ought to make you excited to worship God. A man who won't worship is a man who's not under fatherhood because he can't help it. What is in the father comes to the son.

If you have a trifling father, that's what comes to the son. But, if by the leading of God, you get tied into integrity, tied into power, tied into anointing, then what's in the spiritual father comes down to the son. Jesus said, "Listen, Abraham was excited to see me because Abraham was a father." How do we know that? Every father's goal is to lead his family to God. I'm not talking about a husband. I'm not talking about a male man. Every father's number-one goal is to lead his family to God.

If you choose other things to worship instead of God, you are not a father in God's eyes. If you select the sporting event instead of leading your family to God's House, you are not a father. If your family pursues God and you rely on their relationship with God instead of having a real relationship with God yourself, you are not a father who pleases God. The reason God blessed Abraham is because he led his family to God. Look at how God spoke about Abraham:

"For I know him, that he will command his children and his household after him, and they shall keep the way of the Lord, to do justice and judgment; that the Lord may bring upon Abraham that which he hath spoken of him."

GENESIS 18:19

You might be somebody who struggles in different areas. However, if you want to keep your family blessed, if you want the blessing on your family, make sure you lead them to God. Regardless of the challenges or setbacks, press your way, with your family, to God's House. God says, "I put a blessing on your family."

The reason many of our families are struggling is that we don't have fathers leading their families to God. You are not expected to be a perfect husband or man but, at a minimum, be one who leads your family into God's presence. Your family may be in a broken condition right now. Don't worry about the issues with which you're struggling. Don't worry that you can't seem to please your wife right now.

You might give up on other things, but don't give up on getting your family to God because if you will lead them to God, God will turn around and say, "Now that you led them to me, I bless them." That's what God did for Abraham and that is what He will do for you.

If you will lead your family to the Lord, God will put a blessing on your family. The blessing does not come from working overtime. The blessing does not come from your busyness or endless pursuit of things. These things may help your family but they won't bless your family. Getting them to the House of God will bless your family.

Your family is blessed as you lead them to the Lord, as you get yourself up on Sunday even when you're tired and put your clothes on and say, "As for me and my house, we're going to serve God. Honey, we might have issues and I don't know how to work them out, but this I know: If I lead my family to God, He will bless our family."

This is a consistent Biblical truth. God chastises the Israelites because they are walking in the misguided paths of their fathers.

"Even from the days of your fathers ye are gone away from mine ordinances, and have not kept them. Return unto me, and I will return unto you, saith the Lord of hosts. But ye said, Wherein shall we return?"

MALACHI 3:7

The children of Israel had stopped performing a fundamental spiritual discipline because their fathers before them had stopped doing so. God called on them to return to Him. Here is what God would do in response:

"Bring ye all the tithes into the storehouse, that there may be meat in mine house, and prove me now herewith, saith the Lord of hosts, if I will not open you the windows of heaven, and pour you out a blessing, that there shall not be room enough to receive it."

MALACHI 3:10

We rely upon the blessing of the tithe; however, the tithe is not some mechanical device that produces blessings. God always looks at the heart first.

"And he shall turn the heart of the fathers to the children, and the heart of the children to their fathers, lest I come and smite the earth with a curse."

MALACHI 4:6

Do you see what God did? He spoke about His fatherhood and then called the people back to a relationship with Him.

"A son honoureth his father, and a servant his master: if then I be a father, where is mine honour? and if I be a master, where is my fear? saith the Lord of hosts unto you, O priests, that despise my name. And ye say, Wherein have we despised thy name?"

MALACHI 1:6

"Have we not all one father? hath not one God created us? why do we deal treacherously every man against his brother, by profaning the covenant of our fathers?"

MALACHI 2:10

So, the Book of Malachi speaks more about fatherhood than about tithing. What makes tithing work is that it comes from a heart that honors our Heavenly Father. Tithing is not done out of obligation but out of a real relationship with our Father. In other words, the windows of heaven stay open over a family that tithes and where fatherhood is in the family leading the family to God. Do you want your family blessed? Get yourself in the lead. Teach your family the things of God. You may feel that you are not adequate. That doesn't matter. Get to the house of God and lead your family in the things of God. You may not have a developed prayer life. Pray the best you can. Your family's blessing depends on your leading the way.

"Father" has another meaning. "Father" also means "progenitor." "Progenitor" means to pass on genes. When Adam fell, he not only switched fathers but he switched genes.

"And God said, Let us make man in our image, after our likeness: and let them have dominion over the fish of the sea, and over the fowl of the air, and over the cattle, and over all the earth, and over every creeping thing that creepeth upon the earth. So God created man in his own image, in the image of God created he him; male and female created he them."

GENESIS 1:26

When God created Adam, he made him after His image and likeness. Why? Because God said, "I'll take responsibility to make him like me." A father takes full responsibility to raise up whatever he produces. In other words, if it comes out of me, I'll take responsibility to raise it up. It does not matter if you have challenges with the child's mother; God has called on you to take responsibility for that child and transfer godly DNA to him or her.

"And the Lord God took the man, and put him into the garden of Eden to dress it and to keep it. And the Lord God commanded the man, saying, Of every tree of the garden thou mayest freely eat: but of the tree of the knowledge of good and evil, thou shalt not eat of it: for in the day that thou eatest thereof thou shalt surely die."

GENESIS 2:15

"And when the woman saw that the tree was good for food, and that it was pleasant to the eyes, and a tree to be desired to make one wise, she took of the fruit thereof, and did eat…"

(GENESIS 3:6)

Most bibles have a comma after "she took of the fruit thereof, and did eat,". That comma means we're getting ready to switch gears. When you put in a comma, it's because there's something different that is about to be said. It differs slightly but is still related to the previous topic. It said, "The woman did eat [comma]." Something else took place after the woman ate. In other words, when the woman ate, nothing happened. When the woman ate, the only thing that happened was that it caused the translator to put in a comma. The verse continues:

"…and gave also unto her husband with her; and he did eat. And the eyes of them both were opened…"

Nothing happened until after Adam ate. The woman ate and creation chilled. Adam ate and creation fell. Adam had clear direction from his Father. He was not to touch that tree.

"And the Lord God commanded the man, saying, Of every tree of the garden thou mayest freely eat: But of the tree of the knowledge of good and evil, thou shalt not eat of it: for in the day that thou eatest thereof thou shalt surely die."

GENESIS 2:16-17

One day Adam decided, "I don't want God's opinion anymore." This is where a lot of us are, especially men. Adam decided, "I want to be independent, not interdependent." God never intended for man to be independent of him. He always wanted man to be interdependent with God. Why? Because your identity as a man is tied into your Father. When Eve ate, what happened? Nothing but a comma. Why? Because Eve was not the source. Women did not bring sin into the earth. We spend all our time talking about Eve, what Eve did. The woman could afford to slip because she couldn't bring sin in. She wasn't the source. The source brought it in.

I hope you will receive this revelation. You are the earthly source, and you will reproduce after your own kind. You are a progenitor. You pass on genes, and what you're passing on is who your father is. Whatever is in you is a result of your daddy, and whatever was in your daddy is in you. You pass on your genes. The awesome thing is that just like how Adam, when he fell, got new genes (which were bad genes), when you give your life to the Lord you get a reversal back to heavenly genes.

Adam is considered the earthly source because Adam was the progenitor. Women cannot bring anything forth because they don't have the ability to produce. Men have the ability to produce because we are a source of seed. We are the progenitor. Any time you are not doing the things of God, you are tainting your loins. When Adam ate, everything changed. First, instead of taking responsibility, he began to blame. This was not becoming of a progenitor.

"And they heard the voice of the Lord God walking in the garden in the cool of the day: and Adam and his wife hid themselves from the presence of the Lord God amongst the trees of the garden. And the Lord God called unto Adam, and said unto him,
Where art thou? And he said, I heard thy voice in the garden, and I was afraid, because I was naked; and I hid myself. And he said, Who told thee that thou wast naked? Hast thou eaten of the tree, whereof I commanded thee that thou shouldest not eat? And the man said, The woman whom thou gavest to be with me, she gave me of the tree and I did eat."

GENESIS 3:8-12

Not only did he blame the woman, he blamed God. He said, *"The woman you gave me."* In other words, "If it wasn't for her and if it wasn't for you giving her to me, I wouldn't have done what I did." He became disengaged or detached from fatherhood. Fatherhood takes responsibility and does not shift blame. Fatherhood says, "It's my responsibility." Lack of fatherhood makes excuses.

The second thing that changed is that Adam brought a curse on the ground in all generations after him.

"And unto Adam he said, Because thou hast hearkened unto the voice of thy wife, and hast eaten of the tree, of which I commanded thee, saying, Thou shalt not eat of it: cursed is the ground for thy sake; in sorrow shalt thou eat of it all the days of thy life."

GENESIS 3:17

God said, *"You've eaten of the tree which I commanded you not to eat."* Blame can't go anywhere except to the source. If the family is out of order, it goes to the source. When Adam fell, he switched fathers and genes. The first child he produced resembled the genes that were now in Adam. Who was born? Cain. The Bible says that Cain was hateful, evil, jealous and vindictive. We focus on Cain.

We need to realize that Cain is simply a manifestation of what was in his daddy. His daddy was seeing manifested in front of him what was inside himself. In other words, if you detach from God, your loins have nothing but the ability to produce "Cains."

Women, especially single women, must make sure the men they are interested in have the traits of a true father. If you are single right now and you're with somebody, you must ask to talk with his father. If his father is not saved, if his father doesn't understand fatherhood, the son doesn't understand fatherhood. A man who doesn't understand fatherhood is nothing more than a source who can reproduce all the pain inside him. Single women should desire a man who can walk in the ministry of husband and father. Society has confused the roles within the home but God is very clear.

Husband means lord, master, owner, one with authority or the one you come to get direction from. A husband who has not been fathered will pervert these roles and bring great pain to women. He will verbally and sometimes physically abuse those around him because he has no model to follow. A male man must be fathered in order to walk in the ordained roles of husband and father.

There are two sides that God intended for every man: father and husband. The husband part allows him to kick in and say, "We're going to do this. We're going to do that. We're going to go this way." However, fatherhood nourishes, cherishes, upholds, sustains and maintains. Fatherhood says, "What do *you* think about it?" Fatherhood says, "Honey, what is *your* heart on this?" Fatherhood says, "I'm concerned about how this is going to affect you." You need fatherhood and husband together to have the man of God he is called to be.

On a wedding day, you have a father bringing his daughter down the aisle. The father stops and the pastor says, "Who gives this woman to this man?" The father says, "I do" or "Her mother and I do." At that moment, there is a transfer of responsibility. In other words, as a father, I nourish. I cherish. I protect. I uphold. I will not violate. I will not molest. I will not force her to do anything. If you try to hurt her, you deal with me because I am father. Fatherhood transfers from parental protection to husband protection. Yet here's the problem: Too many fathers have turned their daughters over to men who themselves have not been fathered and who are ignorant about how to properly care for a wife.

It would be better for a woman to stay with her father than to put her life in the hands of a man who lacks the training to be a real husband! A man's money, benefits or career is not enough to fulfill the God-given responsibilities of a husband. A wife must be protected, nourished, cherished, sustained and maintained.

"Husbands, love your wives, even as Christ also loved the church, and gave himself for it; that he might sanctify and cleanse it with the washing of water by the word, that he might present it to himself a glorious church, not having spot, or wrinkle, or any such thing; but that it should be holy and without blemish."

EPHESIANS 5:25

A husband who has been fathered should be able to take off the baggage his wife brings into the marriage. Often, a wife comes into a marriage with baggage because she wasn't under true fatherhood. She may carry the pain of molestation or past abusive relationships. God will use a properly fathered man to bring her to a place of healing. A man will just want to have sex and reproduce but a man who has been fathered will want to bring healing and wholeness to his wife.

A true husband, in response to his wife's baggage, says, "I will cover you and help you discard the baggage. If your baggage has caused you to think that you're ugly or that you're a nobody and no one could ever love you, I'll be your mirror and I'll be your eyes. Look at me and I'll remind you who you are." This is a powerful ministry that a husband offers his wife and it goes beyond physical attraction. As I write this, I can sense that many women who read this will identify with this point. By the prophetic utterance of the Spirit of God, as a father, I speak over your life and break the negative words that have been spoken over you and that have caused you to have the baggage of low self-esteem and insecurity, resulting in a poor self-image. You are made in the image of God and are beautifully, fearfully and wonderfully made. Rise up and be the Woman of God you were destined to be.

God has fashioned the right man for you, one who has been properly fathered so that he will bring healing to every broken place in your life and demonstrate the love of God. This type of man will never exploit your pain or past. He will never constantly criticize his wife. He will love and protect her at all times.

What Paul is really talking about in Ephesians 5 is a husband who has been properly fathered.

"So ought men to love their wives as their own bodies.
He that loveth his wife loveth himself.
For no man ever yet hated his own flesh; but nourisheth and
cherisheth it, even as the Lord the church…"

EPHESIANS 5:28-29

God establishes the standard by which women are to be treated: just like He treats the church. Jesus loves the Church and gave his very life for her! I do not want you to feel condemned because you weren't properly fathered. I want to encourage you! Your ignorance about fatherhood will cause you to make unwise decisions that disrupt your future. God knows how to provide the fatherhood ministry you need.

"A father of the fatherless, and a judge of the widows, is God in his holy habitation."

PSALM 68:5

The moment your earthly father abandoned his responsibility is the exact moment when God stepped in. God will never let you go without a father—both naturally and spiritually.

When a father leaves the home, not only are the children fatherless but the wife is too, and God takes that personally, as we just read in Psalms. God deals with anybody who tries to exploit the fatherless. He takes it personally because he says, "I'm the father now. I'm the protector now. I'm the nourisher now, and if you mess with them, you mess with me." When I was growing up, before my mother was saved, she ran in the streets and brought home different men. It was clear that some of those men meant nothing but bad news for my mother and us. God would intervene and those jokers couldn't stay. God said, "That's my family."

God does this because He wants to protect the purpose that He placed inside each member of the family. If you spend too much time considering those who walked out of your life, you won't recognize how God has stepped in to fill the void.

My stepdad was a drug dealer. One night we returned home and the entire house was ransacked. The intruders pulled guns on us. Another time, while driving in the car, my stepfather—who had a hot temper—got into an altercation with another driver. The other driver pulled out a gun and pointed it at us. I can look back on these things and see how the angels were protecting us. God's mentality, unbeknownst to me back then, was "I have to get that boy grown up because he's going to connect with a fine-looking woman. They're going to start a church and it's going to be called Victory in Christ. They're going to encounter all types of situations. They're going to get knocked down. They're going to get rejected. They're going to get talked about. Everything that happens to them, they're going to make it with my help. I will help them navigate it and then they're going to start a ministry. I'm going to send people who have gone through similar trials and tribulations so that they can break free of hurt, rejection and shame." We have seen God do this! God has taken the hurt and pain that Isha and I experienced and used it to bring healing to God's children.

Many men walk around with unforgiveness in their hearts because their dads walked away. I know what I'm talking about because I was there, walking around with so many questions as a young man. "Why did you leave? How could you leave me? I didn't ask to be here. Why did you leave?" This is what happens: God then tries to send in a father because the seed planter was not the father. If he plants the seed and leaves, he was just a man. If, as a child, your dad left you or was never there, he wasn't a father, he was a seed bearer. As a wife, if your husband left you, he wasn't a father; you must understand that he was just a seed bearer. A true father won't leave his responsibility behind; he will take care of his responsibility.

If you have unforgiveness in your heart, you will reject the father that God sends because you're focusing on what a male seed planter did. You will spend your life trying to prove a point to a male seed planter who couldn't care less about you.

"For if ye forgive men their trespasses, your heavenly Father will also forgive you: But if ye forgive not men their trespasses, neither will your Father forgive your trespasses."

MATTHEW 6:14

If you look in the original Greek, it says, "If you won't forgive, I put you under a curse." The word *curse* means the inability to succeed no matter how hard you try. Every seeming accomplishment is nothing more than a vain attempt to prove to God that you don't need Him. You have unforgiveness in your heart and now you get stagnant because you're under a curse. What sets you free is the revelation of fatherhood and the knowledge that the person who left you didn't have an understanding of themselves; thus, you release them of their ignorance.

Wives who have been truly hurt by their fathers, and maybe even their husbands, must get this revelation as well. You must embrace the fact that they hurt you because they didn't understand fatherhood. If he has hurt you, if he has done things to disappoint you, if he hasn't taken the lead, you must release him because he didn't understand what being a father was all about. It is not about simply bringing home the bacon. It is about nourishing and cherishing and protecting and maintaining and sustaining. Release him and help him get connected to a father who can help him become the father he is called to be.

"I write not these things to shame you, but as my beloved sons
I warn you. For though ye have ten thousand instructors in Christ,
yet have ye not many fathers: for in Christ Jesus
I have begotten you through the gospel."

1 CORINTHIANS 4:14

The church has a father problem because the church has the inability, for the most part, to receive their man and woman of God as a father and mother. You may have been in a church where you didn't have a father; you had instructors. An instructor is there to teach you, and their focus is mainly on seeing you produce or regurgitate what you learned. All they want you to do is show them that you comprehend what you've learned in that class.

Often, you have instructors who teach you and their goal is to see you demonstrate what you have learned. These instructors are not interested in purpose or destiny. A father, on the other hand, does not really focus on what he can get out of you now. A father is looking at raising you up to lead. A father focuses on your purpose, on your destiny and on your calling because he knows there is greatness inside you. An instructor wants you to stay. A father is trying to get you to go. A father understands that if the kid stays too long, it's a perversion because you can't stay home and be 30 and 35 spiritually. A father says, "You're leaving at some point. I'm going to raise you up so that you are ready to go."

The church has a problem because so many times men and women of God who are pastors have an instructor mindset versus a spiritual-father-and-mother mindset. Therefore, they focus on what they can get out of people instead of what they can impart into people so that those people can achieve their destiny. A father will spiritually cut you and prune you. It may cause pain and the immature will sometimes run away from this correction. A spiritual father is more concerned about your development into the person God created and called you to be. A father says, "If I'm your father, you might leave but you'll know I'm your daddy and that I prepared you the best I could. You won't be able to get fathered out there and you'll bring yourself back." A good spiritual father will never say, "I don't want anything to do with you." The father stands with open arms and sees the son or daughter far off and says, "I've been waiting on your return." This is what God has done for us as His children time and time again.

A father celebrates when a child comes back. Why? Because even though that child left in immaturity, they're still the spiritual father's child. You must see your pastor(s) as your spiritual father and mother because you can't receive the fatherhood and motherhood ministry that is in them for you unless you perceive them that way. You may initially struggle with that because you came out of places where church leadership hurt or abused you. Their misbehavior does not change God's plan for his people. The fact that those pastors did not fulfill their God-given function in your life does not mean that God's plan to father you through your pastor has changed. Get into a place where you can trust the man and woman of God and submit to their leadership!

I believe that in this day and age God is fulfilling his prophetic promise of turning the hearts of the children back to their fathers (Malachi 4:6). If the church misses this moment, it will unleash a curse that keeps people bound in mediocrity and outside of God's will for their lives. Purpose emerges only from the fathering process. Jesus didn't come simply for us to receive salvation and go to heaven. He came to restore fatherhood back to the body of Christ. He came to restore men walking in fatherhood. We have all seen the statistics about the absence of fathers and the devastation that ensues. God foresaw that this time would be upon us and that is one of the roles Jesus fulfilled by ushering in a renewed Fatherhood ministry. Unfortunately, the devil has perverted fatherhood with abuse and molestation and other unspeakable acts. God is preparing, by His Spirit, to heal all past wounds so that you can receive the fatherhood ministry.

To every woman, God has made a promise: "I'll put you under biblical fatherhood. I'm not giving you to a man so he can dominate you. My will is that you'll have a man who will cover you, protect you, nourish you and cherish you." If you're carnal-minded, you can't handle this because as a wife you're thinking, 'He won't dominate me.' God never intended for your husband to dominate you. In other words, being submitted under a godly husband who has been properly fathered is for your protection. A properly fathered (natural and spiritual) husband will make an excellent husband. If he really loves God and understands fatherhood, in his role as a husband he will nourish you, protect you, care for you, honor you, maintain you and sustain you.

To my brothers, if you don't get this revelation, your family is headed for a curse because the opposite of fatherhood is fatherlessness. Fatherlessness brings its own curses with it. I recounted some of the effects in the previous chapter. This book is designed to reverse the devastation of fatherlessness by calling men to a new level of fatherhood.

CHAPTER 3

FATHERHOOD
legacy

You don't get to choose to be a male, but you make a choice as to whether you're going to be a father. As you have seen, being a father is very different from simply being a male. A father nourishes, sustains, maintains, provides, protects and upholds those around him. Fatherhood is more than procreation.

"And when Abram was ninety years old and nine,
the Lord appeared to Abram, and said unto him, I am the
Almighty God; walk before me, and be thou perfect. And I will
make my covenant between me and thee, and will multiply thee
exceedingly. And Abram fell on his face: and God talked with him,
saying, As for me, behold, my covenant is with thee, and thou shalt
be a father of many nations. Neither shall thy name any more
be called Abram, but thy name shall be Abraham; for a father of
many nations have I made thee."

GENESIS 17:1-5

Why did God say, "I am the Almighty God"? He was establishing that He can do that which we, as humans, are incapable of doing. This should encourage you! You may not have known your father or you may have had a poor example as a father. You may feel incapable of fulfilling the fatherhood ministry in your family. With

God Almighty, you have hope. You can be who God needs you to be. Wherever you feel inadequate, God makes up the difference. In light of God's ability, He makes a request of Abram. He challenges him to be who he was called to be, which was "perfect"—meaning complete and fulfilled. So, God is saying to Abram, "I am total fulfillment and I expect you to fulfill your destiny by being the father I created you to be."

This is the covenant every father is under. "If you stop being a father, if you stop maintaining, nourishing, providing and protecting, I stop being almighty God to you." This is why God changed Abram's name. God wanted Abram to completely embrace his calling to be a father so he was called Abraham from that day.

For men, there is a point at which you embrace your destiny as a father. Even if your name does not formally change, there is an inward change and an acknowledgement of a divine calling. A man must choose to be the father God created him to be. This is intentional and not a coincidence. Fatherhood, then, is a covenant between God and men. Every man will not accept this covenant; those who do will miss experiencing the blessing of Almighty God.

I pray that you, as a man, will accept your calling to the Fatherhood ministry that God put within you. This is not about procreation. It's far bigger than that. A man who has embraced his fatherhood destiny will pour into those around him and will seek the best for them, regardless of whether a biological connection exists. God requires fathers to take responsibility to cover those around them. A father will always cover his family. As long as you cover your family, God says, "What you can't do, I'll do." In other words, "You just cover. I've got your back. When you hit a situation in which you don't know what to do, as long as you stay in the cover position concerning your family, I will be Almighty God to you. What you can't do, I'll do."

Fatherhood as progenitor determines the quality of life for the whole family. Again, that word "progenitor" means, "in front of ancestry." In other words, if the father is not covering and taking responsibility, the quality of life for that family is lessened. A father who does not take fatherhood seriously affects the life of that family, and he is affecting the life of three to four generations after him.

Every boy is a progenitor because he has seed within him. Every male affects the generations coming behind him because of his ability to pass on seed. Women can't pass on seed because they don't have seed. Women just carry seed. In other words, women receive what is given to them. They receive it, incubate it, multiply it and give it back. As a husband, if you plant your seed in your wife, she incubates it, multiplies it and gives you back a baby. This is not just a sexual principle. If a husband gives his wife frustration, she receives it, incubates it, multiplies it and gives it back in torment and nagging. If a husband gives his wife a lack of financial stability, she'll incubate it, multiply it and give it back in the form of stress and fear. But if you give her stability, if you give her vision, if you give her leadership, if you give her direction, if you give her guidance, she will incubate it, multiply it and give it back in peace and submission. In other words, she will help you get to where you are going. The question is… *What are you giving her to work with?*

I want to show you in the Scripture that women have no capability of passing on sin. Only men pass on sin. Every man has the ability to pass on sin. In other words, generational curses never came from a woman; they came from men. Men are the only people who have the ability to pass on generational curses to the third or fourth generation. What you do right now passes down to three and four generations. If you abandon your family, the shockwaves will be felt for three and four generations. If you remain at home but refuse to be the man God calls you to be, the model you set will affect three to four generations.

If God is not a priority in your family, if you won't lead your family in the things of God, if you don't lead them to church, if church isn't a priority, you are not only affecting the quality of life of *your* family, you are passing spiritual seed down to three or four generations of men who don't know who they are.

"Thou shalt not bow down thyself to them, nor serve them: for I the Lord thy God am a jealous God, visiting the iniquity of the fathers upon the children unto the third and fourth generation of them that hate me; And shewing mercy unto thousands of them that love me, and keep my commandments."

EXODUS 20:5-6

That word *visiting* is the Hebrew word *paqad*, which means "to charge with and punish." These verses do not mention mothers! The word *iniquity* is the Hebrew word *'avon*, which means "to intentionally do wrong." Let's tie it together. "I'm a jealous God, and I charge with and punish the intentional wrong of the fathers..." But where is this visited? Upon the children up to four generations beyond. God says, "I charge your wrong to the children coming behind you. That doesn't mean you get away scot-free, but that does mean it's not just about you." The actions you take right now will not affect only you. Others will most definitely be touched. That's what we call a generational curse.

Fathers who reject the covenant of fatherhood will pass down a covering of failure for three to four generations. It is essential that men take into consideration this vital point as they live their lives. Their actions will not affect just the immediate family but generations. With one bit of the forbidden fruit, Adam changed all of humanity. If one man can negatively affect three and four generations, what would happen if just the men who read this book took a stand for fatherhood, stayed with their families and walked in their rightful place? We could heal a whole society of men who say, "I will not affect four generations negatively. I'll bless a thousand generations."

Think about it this way. Today you are experiencing either the blessing or the curse from your great-grandfather's actions. This should cause each person reading this book to examine his private life and the secrets he keeps. These secrets, though unknown to those around you, will most definitely affect them and their progeny. The things you struggle with today may stem from a previous generation's inability to overcome a habit or addiction. On the other hand, every act of righteousness will impute the blessings of God to successive generations.

I have counseled men over the years who don't fully understand this. They come to me seeking help because they struggle with issues in their personal lives. They attribute this to the devil or demons when in actuality it is nothing more than the manifestation of a generational curse. When you are dealing with a generational curse, you must renounce and denounce all previous generational associations. To *renounce* means "to speak against." *Denounce* is a term that means "to forgive or remove from position." Generational curses must be spoken against and the effects declared forgiven and removed from the person's life. You may want to pause right now to renounce and denounce certain ungodly behaviors like lying, unfaithfulness, dishonesty or any other persistent hindrance in your life. To every man who is struggling with things he can't seem to shake, if you have not renounced what was let in, you must say, *"In the Name of Jesus, I renounce every sin, every iniquity, every negative thing my great-grandfather did. Every time my great-grandfather didn't walk with God—if he never walked with God—I denounce the ungodliness. I denounce the generational curses that have been passed down in my life. I declare, 'No more!' I denounce it. No more in my life, in my family's life. No more! It stops right here, right now. I'm the righteousness of God, and I renounce and denounce everything that family before me did to pass down generational curses. From this day forward it ends. In Jesus' Name."*

Now, I want you to understand what began to take place in the spiritual, unseen realm as a result of what you just declared. The Bible says that when you speak, what you say begins to happen. As you began to utilize your legal right to denounce, the angels that are assigned to you, that haven't heard you say anything in years, shouted, "Finally!" The Bible says you have angels assigned to you to minister to you as an heir of salvation (Hebrews 1:14). Your band of angels has been dispatched. They are on the move now, coming against generational curses, coming against negative things, moving and shaking. Spiritual warfare is happening. The angels are responding to the words you spoke. Now when negative thoughts try to influence you to continue in negative generational activity, you can declare, *"I spoke against that. You have no right to even come here."*

Understand that the enemy will fight a man who desires to break these generation chains because the enemy knows how powerful a man is who has a fatherhood mentality. When a man takes the step to walk in God's fatherhood ministry, he will need love and support from those around him. No man gets fatherhood right every time. However, it is a blessing to know that those around the man are supportive of his journey and will serve to encourage him along the way. I urge the women, and even children, who are reading this book to not criticize, demean or undermine what God is doing in this man's life. He will not be perfect but with God's guidance and your support, he will become the father who is pleasing in God's sight. Pray every day for this man to walk boldly in the fatherhood ministry and be the covering that God is calling him to be.

Use your words to commend him and speak life to him! Confess over his life the promises of God, in the present tense—not the future tense. Faith is now! Your confession should never be "My husband will fulfill the fatherhood ministry" This is expectation and hope. Faith says, "My husband fulfills the fatherhood ministry." Confess that your husband leads your family after God's heart. Confess that he is a mighty man of God. You will receive resistance from the devil but don't let that stop you. Don't allow your mouth to agree with the devil's plan to hurt your husband.

The next step to support a man in embracing the fatherhood mantle is to show him honor throughout the process. Regardless of how he misses the mark, you have a mandate from God to build him up. Do not tell others about your husband's actions. When you speak negatively about your husband, you are stepping from under his covering. Also, please do not talk negatively about your spouse to single people around you. They will offer you advice that has never been tested—which could be why they are still single.

You should honor him whether or not he deserves it. I don't care if he doesn't take out the trash. I don't care if he doesn't wash the dishes. I don't care if he says he'll be home at 10:00 and he's not there until 11:30. You honor him. What are you doing? You're honoring him by faith. Whatever he's not doing, you speak and honor it as if it's so. Say things like this: "I honor you. You're a man of integrity. You're a man who balances the bills. You're a man who leads our family. I honor you." Even if his actions do not align with these words, keep speaking them. You will see a change! He may not deserve it but he needs these words to push him to keep moving forward. The honor you sow into his life will pay great future dividends. When you have seen your husband acting out of his generational curse, he is acting on a lie from the devil. You should remember that the devil is and always has been a liar.

"Ye are of your father the devil, and the lusts of your father ye will do. He was a murderer from the beginning, and abode not in the truth, because there is no truth in him. When he speaketh a lie, he speaketh of his own: for he is a liar, and the father of it. And because I tell you the truth, ye believe me not."

JOHN 8:44

You may be frustrated by your husband's actions but don't cooperate with the devil's plan to destroy him and your family. Honor your husband and pray for him regardless of what he's doing because what he's battling is the legacy his great-grandfather left.

Until he read this book, he may not even have known that he was fighting a generational curse. Men are so proud. We're tough, and we don't want to share with anybody the fact that we are struggling. We think we have it all together. As frustrated as you are by his actions, he's frustrated too. He might not show it to you. He might not tell you, but he's frustrated because he knows you are right. Everybody is struggling with what their great-grandfather did. That doesn't mean you throw your hands up and give up. You're supposed to do something about it. Renounce it. Denounce it. Take a stand.

My wife and I come from messed-up families. In our families, there are all types of bad behaviors that have run rampant. Divorce, drugs, alcohol, sex outside of marriage, abuse, physical abuse, all types of craziness. We took a stand, and it started with me. Our boys will never see a family broken up. Our boys will never see Daddy out of the house. Regardless of what happens, I'm not going anywhere. If somebody is leaving, it isn't going to be me. If my wife tries to leave, I'll pray for her to stay. There will be no addictions from past forefathers because we renounced those past things. We did a machine-gun renouncing. "In the name of Jesus, every foul thing that is our family lineage, we renounce and take authority over you." We went item by item in our families. It was so liberating.

The first time I went hunting, I received a revelation on how real things are in our family. I'd never fired a gun in my life. The person I was with gave me his brand-new high-powered rifle and was teaching me how to hold it. You're supposed to put the butt of the rifle into the section of your shoulder right between where your chest ends and your shoulder begins. This proper positon helps minimize the kick back from firing the rifle. Once I understood the proper positon, he said, "Do some target practice." He said, "See that rock out there?" It was way out, like 400 yards away, next to a tree. He said, "Hit the rock next tree on the left." I got the scope of the rifle on the rock, I aimed and I hit the rock. The person I was with said, "Have you ever shot a gun before?" I said, "No. It's in my family, though. I have some shooters up in my family." Even though I had never fired a gun before, I received as a legacy the ability to handle firearms/rifles with skill. As we began to hunt for live game, I learned a powerful lesson from the deer. In a dangerous situation, the buck sends his family out front and waits behind the protection of the trees. He emerges only after the doe and fawn have gone ahead. The experienced hunter told me that in the animal kingdom, males will string out the rest of the family. So it is with our species as well; if a man doesn't understand fatherhood, he'll possibly string out his family, let them get hurt and then, after the dust clears, he'll want to go on his way.

It's supposed to be the other way around. It's supposed to be that the husband, the father, leads the way and when danger comes, he keeps his family safe at all costs. Every man reading this book should be the last one going to bed. You should lock the doors. Please don't tell your wife, "Lock up before you come up." No, no, no. If she stays up later, you still secure the house. Put the alarm on. Lock the windows. If you hear something creak in the house, don't send her down. If you won't take the lead, you are just like that buck standing in the back, allowing his family to walk into harm's way.

The Enemy waits for an uncovered family. If the family is uncovered, in hunting terms, he doesn't even need a scope to get them. He can take down an uncovered family. In a family that is covered, the devil may shoot but he won't be able to hit anyone because fatherhood invokes Almighty God's protective powers.

The Holy Spirit has been assigned by Jesus to lead and guide you to reestablish fatherhood in the earth (John 16:13). As the man in the fatherhood position goes throughout life, the Holy Spirit leads and guides this regenerated man. The Holy Spirit will lead the man even when he makes mistakes and missteps. The Holy Spirit will lead the man to the right woman to marry. God will give that man clear direction on how to cover his family and leave a godly legacy.

If you are a woman who has experienced the negative effects of a broken man, I want you to know that God has not forgotten about you. He is still your Heavenly Father and he will cover, protect, provide and nourish you. This is why I spoke of honor earlier. You can honor your husband even when he is not doing everything you know God has told him to do because you know that God is the one who can perfect His work in your husband. You never want to stand in the way of God's work. Your diligent confession and honor will give God room to work in your husband's life and make him a father after God's own heart. God will even restore him after he makes mistakes. God can heal a broken family so long as the wife does not get offended and become carnally-minded. Your husband is God's child, even if he doesn't acknowledge it. God will work in response to your confession! Don't believe the lie of the devil that you are better off without your husband. Even in cases of abuse, I have seen God heal this after a time of separation for the man to get the help he needed. I am saddened when I see a woman reject God's ability to heal her situation. Unfortunately, a broken man can bring a great deal of hurt to a family. However, if he is able to bring a great amount of devastation, he can also bring a great number of blessings when he is walking in destiny as a father. God can and will bring your family back together. It may take some time.

When God brings that man back, the wife must be willing to relinquish that leading role she assumed when the man left. Role reversal will collapse a family because God never intended for a woman to carry the load of the family. To try and operate this way is a perversion of the order and will of God as it pertains to the family. To not allow fatherhood to operate even after he has fallen but has been restored goes against the covenant order of God. We saw earlier that God says, "My covenant is with fatherhood, and if there's fatherhood in the house I bless the house."

If the father is not there or refuses to be restored, God still steps in to care for the family. This is where the blessing of God is. When you have a husband, a father, who's maintaining, sustaining, protecting and guiding the family, and the family is in order and the family is right, God's covenant purpose for family is being upheld in the earth.

Even if you left your family, when God restores you, He expects you to take your rightful place and stand guard over your family, ready to fight the enemy when he tries to rear his ugly head. A father stands in the gap as the head of the house and conducts spiritual warfare. What is on the line is a godly legacy of blessings or a demonic legacy of brokenness and pain. The man who aligns with God's ministry of fatherhood will cancel past generational curses and release perpetual generational blessings.

CHAPTER 4

FATHERS
give & sustain
LIFE

FATHERS
give & sustain
LIFE

N ow that we have established a true understanding of fatherhood for both men and women, let's move into the specific functions of a father. We mentioned in the beginning of this book that the highest calling of a man is fatherhood. No salary, career, title or accolade compares to the fatherhood calling. To fully understand fatherhood, one must comprehend the functions of a father. I believe that there are 10 functions that a real, God-ordained father performs for those in his life. Throughout the first three chapters, I've generally referenced some of these but I have not gone into detail. The next several chapters will elaborate on these roles and responsibilities so that there is no confusion as to God's expectations for men who walk in the fatherhood calling.

The first function of a father is that of *life-giver.*

"And hath made of one blood all nations of men for to dwell on all the face of the earth, and hath determined the times before appointed, and the bounds of their habitation; That they should seek the Lord, if haply they might feel after him, and find him, though he be not far from every one of us: For in him we live, and move, and have our being; as certain also of your own poets have said, For we are also his offspring."

ACTS 17:26-28

God used one man to create all humanity. God created Adam, and Adam was designed to give life to other humans. God remains the source and Adam was given the responsibility of being fruitful and multiplying on the earth. Adam was the first human father. Even though the flood occurred and all humanity was destroyed except for Noah, Noah can trace his lineage back to Adam. Through one man and one bloodline, all the nations of the earth came forth. This is a reference to Adam's role in giving life to all humanity. God appointed Adam to function in this way. However, Adam was not given complete autonomy. The Scripture continues by saying that God *"...hath determined the times before appointed, and the bounds of their habitation..."* While Adam gives life, God retains the sole right to determine the bounds and the times of humanity. So, God sets the ends before anything begins. Before any person appeared on earth, God established when and where you would live. That means wherever you are right now, God knows it. Even though you might feel like nobody knows where you are, God knows where you are because according to what we're reading, He determined your existence before you existed.

Before you arrived on earth, God not only determined your existence, He determined your outcome before your existence began. No matter where you are in life right now, God has already been there, knew what was going to happen to you, and created a way of escape that you might be able to bear it before you even got on this planet.

> *"There hath no temptation taken you but such as is common to man: but God is faithful, who will not suffer you to be tempted above that ye are able; but will with the temptation also make a way to escape, that ye may be able to bear it."*

1 CORINTHIANS 10:13

God has not only provided your escape from bad situations, He will also guide your steps.

*"The steps of a good man are ordered by the Lord:
and he delighteth in his way."*

PSALM 37:23

You can walk with confidence knowing that God is not only guiding your steps but that He also knows the path to your destiny. All this is so that you can come to know God better. This is all God has ever wanted—His creation to be in relationship with Him. God also reminds us that He is not far from any of us.

God is not far from any one of us, even though we might feel it. This clarifies a back theological mindset we possess. We think that God is so mysterious that He is hard to find and hard to understand. That could not be further from the truth. God wants us to find Him and have a relationship with Him. Whatever you are going through or wherever you may be, God will use it to bring you closer to Him.

God's goal when you are on this planet is for you to find your way back to where you once were—with Him. A father's role is to help those to whom he has given life find the God who is the source of life! A man walking in true fatherhood not only gives life but also leads his offspring to eternal life. You know that you were made in God's image and nothing in God's image can be bad! Your life is uniquely fashioned to show forth the goodness and beauty of God. God set your path, orders your steps and knows the finish line for your life. A father is crucial in helping you find God so that you can walk the path God has set before you.

Even though the first function of a father is to give life, that is only the beginning. Still, notice how the world has watered down the functions that God has assigned to the father. The world has said that fatherhood is established by this one criterion. However, even the role of a life-giver is led by God, as He is the one who established the times and the boundaries of each human life. The role of father as life-giver is conducted under the leadership of God, who is not concerned only about the beginning of life but every stage of life. In God's eyes, men and women are the same except that the male man gives seed and the female man receives and incubates seed (Genesis 1). Beyond these biological differences, God gives divine functions that each performs in conjunction with His larger purposes. When a man inseminates a woman in the world's eyes, he is a father. However, in God's eyes that man is operating at the beginning stages of manhood. When that man accepts responsibility for the life he helped create and provides direction, he has started to walk down God's path of Fatherhood. There are clear biological distinctions between the man and the woman.

Women can never be a source because they don't have seed. Men can never be an incubator because they do not have a womb. We must be mindful of this. Even though society attempts to redefine gender identification, it is very clear in God's eyes. Even if the woman makes more money than the man or has more education than the man, she cannot be the life-giver.

It takes both male and female to produce offspring. Each gender has its unique role to play in God's creative plan. This is the central point of why homosexuality and same-sex marriages are wrong in the sight of God. Those marriages cannot produce the intended purpose of God of seed being given to be incubated, multiplied and reproduced in the earth.

This male man is the life-giver (initiator). The initiator needs an incubator for seed. Seed will die without an incubator. The incubator can't carry the seed if there's no seed put inside. The incubator needs the initiator for seed and the initiator needs the incubator. God says, "Both of you need each other." If that is a true principle in the natural, we need to understand in the spirit as well. Whatever the initiator plants in the incubator, that's what she's going to incubate, multiply and give back. If the initiator initiates a seed of frustration, the incubator automatically incubates that inside. Anything that goes inside the incubator is going to multiply. It will multiply itself and give back. If there is frustration in your house, it is not the incubator's fault; it's the initiator's. The incubator cannot initiate anything. The incubator can do nothing more than receive what is being planted. If there are financial problems in a marriage, it is going back to the initiator because the incubator can only bring forth what was planted inside her. Do you see how God's order works in both the natural and spiritual realms?

Men don't like to hear this but there is a great responsibility on the man as a life-giver. Whenever there is a problem in the home, it traces back to the life-giver (initiator). The wife only carries what has been given to her. If the husband wants different results, he must sow different seed. The incubator can carry only what was initiated from the start. Whatever problems are in a house, the incubator must point to the problem. The initiator has no business pointing anywhere except himself.

God has made the male man the life-giving source. He's the initiator of everything. If the male man is the initiator, he must be very mindful of the ground in which he's going to plant his seed. He must make sure the ground is fully prepared so that it will produce the proper harvest. In other words, he must make sure the seed has a sign on it saying, "Approved by God." This makes the dating/courting process much more serious because there are significant spiritual ramifications when initiator and incubator come together.

I know this is a metaphor but the woman you desire to join in marriage must have God's seal of approval on her. This will let you know that the soil is quality. Look for warning signs because sometimes God will label a woman "radioactive" and you certainly want to stay away from that type of woman, regardless of how beautiful she may look. If she is not a believer or has destructive behaviors, she's bad soil right now. This advice is true for the woman as well. When a man enters your life, see if he has God's seal of approval on him.

If bad seed (initiator) enters good ground (incubator), it will produce a negative harvest. It is a law! Bad seed into good soil will yield bad fruit. I've counseled too many women who used the wrong criteria to select an initiator and they regret it. They used looks, financial status and the opinions of others to select a husband. However, those man did not have God's approval on their lives. A father's first function is to serve as a life-giver (initiator).

The second function of fatherhood is to be a *sustainer*. God is very clear about His expectations for the husband/father in this regard. After God created everything, he gave the man a specific instruction.

"And the Lord God took the man,
and put him into the garden of Eden
to dress it and to keep it."

GENESIS 2:15

God's assignment to Adam was to "dress and keep" the Garden which God created. The word *dress* means "to sustain or work." The first thing God gave the man was not a woman but a job. Before the woman arrived on the scene, God placed the man in the garden and instructed him, "Work the garden." In other words, God said, "Show me that you can take care of what's been given to you." Single ladies, do you see the man who is pursuing you as capable of taking care of himself before he can take care of you? If he can't take care of himself, what would make you think he can take care of you? Whatever he cannot maintain by himself, he will not maintain when he's married to you. This mistake is made too many times in marriage. Yes, you should marry potential but if a man cannot demonstrate that he has a strong work ethic, he is not ready to be a husband or a father. If he looks to you as a provider or sustainer, he has a distorted view of his God-given role in the relationship.

God knows how to give you the correct mate. Counterfeits may present themselves. Single women in particular must make sure that God has sent the men they are dating. Don't prematurely commit your life to someone who does not have a fundamental understanding of the importance of work. If you wait to find out later, you may be sorely disappointed. God is not going to give you away to a man who will not take responsibility and who will not work. God will never confirm a man who does not meet His standards of Fatherhood. And you, as a woman, should have an internal witness that this man meets the Biblical criteria to be your husband. I plead with you: Do not rush into marriage without a strong confirmation that the man meets God's standards.

Every man must have a garden experience. When God put the man in the garden, there was nothing there to distract him from being in God's presence. God put the man in the garden before he had any other responsibilities. God put the man in the garden to be in God's presence. Every man must have a garden experience. It is desired and preferable that a man have his garden experience *before* he is married. This is the order of God. Of course, God will transform men after marriage but it is far more difficult. I liken it to trying to change the tires on a moving car. It is easier to change the tires when the car is stopped. Trying to make this major adjustment after marriage is a challenge and very disruptive. The male man must be in God's presence so he can learn how to be a good father. In God's presence, without the distraction of a wife and children, God teaches Adam (the man) how to be a nurturer, a cherisher, a sustainer.

God put the man in the garden so he could learn how to take care of anything entrusted to him. Adam had God as a personal mentor to show him how to be the man God desired him to be. This was invaluable development time. As Adam worked, I can imagine God correcting him and showing him how to care for the garden properly. I can imagine God patting Adam on the back and telling him that he did a great job. All this was an intentional process that God used to teach Adam how to become a sustainer. Once Adam learned how to sustain himself and that around him, he would be ready for the greatest assignment he could be given: to care for Eve, his wife.

If you're married and your husband has not had a garden experience, you may encounter challenges. When a man lacks a garden encounter, he won't have a prayer life or a work ethic. He needs both because his work is an extension of his ministry assignment. If you have a man who does not spend time with God daily, ask God to show you how to encourage him in this area. What would it be worth to you if you husband did not have as many "Honey Do" items so that he could spend time with God? Maybe you could ask him, if he's willing, to spend time with God together. Every man must learn how to be in God's presence. I can't be a father without spending time with *the* Father. The problem is that in our marriages we have fathers who can't operate in fatherhood because they're not spending time with *the* Father. A single man, before he gets married, must spend time in the presence of God so that he can learn about his purpose and fatherhood. If a man does not know his purpose, when he gets married and when children arrive, that man will be just as lost as his wife and children. If the man lacks focus and purpose, the entire home will struggle. It is rough being a man but God built you to take it. Men are physically stronger than women from the waist up.

Man of God, you are built to handle the roughness. You're built to handle the toughness. When things get out of line and out of whack, you're built to handle it. As a matter of fact, the rougher it gets, the more you're able to thrive under pressure. My desire for you after you read this book is that not only will you, as a man, know who you are but you'll also realize that you're able to handle the pressure.

"But if any provide not for his own, and specially for those of his own house, he hath denied the faith, and is worse than an infidel."

1 TIMOTHY 5:8

The word *infidel* means "Unbeliever." How could it get any worse than being an unbeliever? God says that for a man who does not take care of his family, it is as if he has denied the faith. He is worse than an unbeliever. When you research the word "infidel," you'll see that the definition ends with "the final outcome being hell." So, if a man who does not support his family is *worse* than an infidel, that state is worse than hell! This is such a fundamental instruction from God. Research has shown that one of the key causes of divorce is financial issues. Financial pressures wear the family down. When there is out-of-control spending and a lack of income, it can break a family. As the sustainer, the husband should bring clarity to the family's finances to ensure that the budget is balanced and all bills are paid.

No woman should marry a deficit (financial or otherwise). A deficit is anything that will detract from who you are and what God has installed in you prior to marriage. If, as a woman, you are thriving and doing well for God, why would you want to submit to a man who is in a deficit situation (spiritually and financially)? A deficit causes you to regress to a lower level. If you look at that man who is supposed to be father and he can't help you get to another level, you're stepping into union with a deficit. When God gives you a man, he should already be operating as a father, which means he's a cultivator like *the* Father and will satisfy any deficit before marriage so that the union will be stronger after marriage.

Jesus masters satisfying deficits. This is why a man who spends time with Jesus is an ideal candidate for husband/father because he will not allow deficits. You may recall the woman with the issue of blood. She came to Jesus seeking to have a deficit reversed. She had done everything within her own power and her situation had grown worse. Isn't this what we do? We try to solve our most pressing situations with our own wisdom and it usually does not go well. When she released her faith and decided to meet Jesus, she knew her situation would change. And, it did! Jesus didn't just heal her, he made her whole!

One question you can use to ascertain your suitor's readiness to be a sustainer is to ask him to share what God has been saying to him about his life and future. This is not a question about his salvation experience but his relationship status with God. How has God been guiding and directing his life on a daily basis?

If the man pursuing you doesn't have a tangible, true relationship with God, you are setting yourself up for a very real deficit. This is not meant as an insult to men! It is setting the bar higher so that our men will rise up to fulfill what God established from the beginning of creation. Fatherhood can truly be fatherhood only if there is intimate fellowship with the Heavenly Father. Why? Because true fatherhood that spends time with the God of Fatherhood will be anointed to remove burdens and destroy yokes within the context of a marriage.

Man of God, you are more anointed than any pastor to pray for your wife because you're the one with the anointing to remove any burden and destroy any yoke in her life. I know churches have told you differently. "Bring her to me," the pastor may say, but the pastor doesn't have the anointing to remove a burden and destroy a yoke off your wife. *You* have it. What the pastor should do is tell you, "You go, lay hands on your wife and cast out the devil." You don't need to know any Hebrew or Greek words. All you need to know is two words: "Come out." Anointing doesn't have a look; it just is. Men, you don't have to look a certain way. If you have spent time with God, you are anointed. In a family, that father, that husband is the one who is anointed to remove every burden and destroy every yoke. It's time for you to step into your rightful place and be a father.

A man ready to walk in true fatherhood will never have premarital sex. Of course, he will desire it but he knows that the act of sex before marriage would taint his relationship and remove God's hand from the relationship. It is that time with God that keeps those sexual urges in control. If you are cohabitating or actively having sexual relations outside of marriage, you are not taking the responsibility of fatherhood seriously. A man who walks in the fatherhood ministry would never want to defile his wife because, ultimately, she is God's daughter.

The same is true of a woman who entices a man to sleep with her before marriage. You are establishing a pattern that will harm your marriage because the man will lose respect for you—especially if you confess that you follow Jesus. You are creating a deficit in your relationship which will carry over into your marriage. You must refuse to drop your standards or give yourself to anybody short of your husband.

At the time of the writing of this book, my wife and I have been married for 25 years. Even after 25 years of marriage, that girl has my nose so wide you could run a truck up through that thing. I love that woman. I'll mess you up over her. I get chills just thinking about her. Your marriage is supposed to be awesome and exciting; you can't wait to be around your spouse. We have kept the passion in our relationship because we have honored our roles and never frustrated the grace of God or done something to remove the hand of God from our marriage. I didn't have a father to show me what to do but I got hooked up with *the* Father. I had my garden experience, and I want my boys to have the example before them that I never had. I'm working on something. I'm instructing my boys when they see their dad grab their mom's hand. I'm training my boys when they see their dad love their mom unconditionally. I'm modeling being an attentive husband when my boys see their dad offer their mom compliments in public. I'm creating generational blessings! I'm working on my seed and my seed's seed. God said, "If you'll be a godly father to them, I'll be Almighty God to you." I don't have time to worry about what people think I should or should not do. I want to impact generations. Fathers, please heed these words. You have the ability to change generations. Your wife can't do it. Only you can do it. You have seed that you can pass down.

CHAPTER 5

FATHERS
PROTECT

The revelation presented in this book terrifies the devil. When a man understands his true role in life and boldly walks in that role, he will take back territory that the devil has held for far too long. I am committed to the goal that for every family the devil has attacked, I want to rescue 10! I've made up my mind to spend my days restoring men to their rightful place.

The third function of a father is *protector*. Let's revisit Genesis 2:15.

"And the Lord God took the man, and put him into the garden of Eden to dress it and to keep it."

We discussed what it meant to dress the garden. However, God gave another assignment to Adam, "to keep it." The word *keep* means "to guard and protect." That's the third function. The father is a protector. These responsibilities were assigned to the man in the absence of a woman. And I want to make this clear: A man should not do these things to win a woman! He should do these things to please God. The overflow of pleasing God will result in the right woman appearing in his life but not before these three manifest. These three things God required of Adam before Eve showed up. In the same manner, God requires them of any man before he is ready to have a wife. I have listened to women tell my wife that they believed an unsaved, irresponsible, unemployed man was the one God sent them. As much as my wife would try to dissuade a woman from this bad decision, the woman's desperation to be married blinded her to these deficiencies. Down the road, those same women would return to my wife and bemoan the fact that they had made a mistake. It is too late to ask for help after you have married a man who lacks the fathering of God.

Before God put the woman in the garden, he told the man, "Now you're going to learn how to protect what I've given you." The man must learn how to protect everything and everyone under his care. If a man doesn't learn to protect his wife prior to her arrival, he will abuse her when she gets there. It may be physically, verbally, emotionally or a combination. If he does not know how to protect those connected to him, his wife and children will suffer. A man who is not a protector will always fight for himself and leave everyone around him to fend for themselves (similar to that buck I talked about in a previous chapter). All he has learned to do is defend himself. When he feels like you're attacking him, he'll defend himself against you.

Fatherhood understands that the wife could never really attack you. When she's expressing frustration, a man who walks in the fatherhood ministry understands that this comes from a place of vulnerability. The man won't attack the wife but he will assuage her concerns so that her frustration lessens. A godly husband will not verbally assault his wife or demean her in any way. A true father nourishes, cherishes, maintains and sustains under pressure. A well-fathered man knows that he is built to handle whatever arises within his relationship. He will protect his house! So, what does God expect the man to protect?

The first thing God gives the man to protect is his Word. This is why sustainer comes before protector. Once the man has spent time with God, he will cherish that relationship and God's Word. He will make sure God's Word is not compromised in his life or his family. If a man can't protect God's Word, he can't protect his wife and children.

*"My son, attend to my words; incline thine ear unto my sayings.
Let them not depart from thine eyes; keep them in the midst
of thine heart. For they are life unto those that find them, and
health to all their flesh."*

That word *attend* means "to do your job and take care of." Your job is to take care of the Word of God over your family. If a man is going to protect his family, he must learn how to speak the Word over his family. If your wife or your children are sick, you must learn how to speak the Word. Speak the Word concerning their healing, your finances and their purpose. The greatest protection a man offers his family is the spiritual protection that comes from declaring God's Word over the household. God's Word should remain in your mouth and heart so that it is on a quick trigger when a problem arises. When you are under attack, that is not the time to try to find a Scripture. You protect your family with the Word.

If his family is under attack from sickness, the well-fathered man will reject that diagnosis and speak forth God's healing power. The husband speaks God's Word over his wife and children, or he speaks the Word over his own body. If your children are not performing academically at the level you know they should, speak the Word over them. Because you have creative power, if you speak negativity over your wife or children, it will manifest in their lives. Speak life which is God's Word. This is not a task that can be delegated to the wife or the pastor. The spiritual father of the home is the man! His word is authoritative in the house. What the man says causes heaven to move. You should never let your family leave the house without declaring God's protecting power over their lives. It doesn't have to be a long prayer but you should not leave them unprotected as they interact with the world. Remember, your wife can follow or incubate only what you initiate. In the context of marriage, if you don't lead it, there's no anointing on her to follow. If you don't initiate speaking the Word within the context of family, there is no anointing on her to speak it because she's an incubator.

When you're single it's different because you're the head of the house. When you're married, you'd better make sure you have a man who speaks that Word. If you're married right now and he's not speaking it, that's the time to get help. This is where the wife's encouragement ministry should start. Ask him to speak the Word over you. Even if he doesn't know Scripture, you as the wife can find the Scriptures, print them out and ask him to declare them over you daily. A man who will speak the Word over his family is a man who is protecting his family. You cannot protect your family if, in the difficult moments, you use your mouth as an offensive weapon against your family members or you speak words of defeat and frustration. As a man whom God has fathered, or a man whom God desires to father, you can handle whatever comes your way. You have all it takes if you just lean into your destiny as a protector.

If it looks like your family is drowning, don't allow your mouth to cooperate with your defeat. Speak forth the Word of God over your family and watch God turn it around. Like those who are familiar with the military, a good soldier never leaves his post. Once you say, "I do," you are on assignment until death do you part. Every day you are on protective detail for your family. For anybody to get to your family, they must get through you. If the Enemy wants to attack your family, he must come through you—and God.

God formed you to be strong and courageous. God has called you as a man to be the father of your house, to stand strong, to stand mightily and to be the man of God he has called you to be. You can do it! You're a warrior. You're a man of God. You're anointed for your situation. You stand and protect your family against the wiles of the devil. It doesn't matter what your struggle may be. Stand strong. If you stand strong, the things you're struggling with will begin to melt away like butter because you're operating in fatherhood. God knows that you are not perfect but He knows that His Word will perfect you! If you keep declaring his Word over your life, He will deliver you from those secret hindrances. Your family will never improve until you improve! You are not just a man, you are a man of God who protects the Word!

You need to understand something. God has directed this book into your hands so that you will know once and for all who you were created to be. You're a man of God. If you're married, you must get it together quickly. If you're single, don't start a relationship until you are eligible based upon the Word of God. You need to be man enough to say, "I can't help you right now. I'll mess you and myself up. I must prepare myself so I can lead my family." When you take a stand for fatherhood, the devil will attack you like he did with Jesus in the desert. What he told Jesus is what he tries to tell you. I know there are men reading this book whom the enemy has deceived into thinking that they are inadequate. To every lie from the devil, you have the Word to respond!

"Then was Jesus led up of the Spirit into the wilderness to be tempted of the devil. And when he had fasted forty days and forty nights, he was afterward an hungred. And when the tempter came to him, he said, If thou be the Son of God, command that these stones be made bread. But he answered and said, It is written, Man shall not live by bread alone, but by every word that proceedeth out of the mouth of God. Then the devil taketh him up into the holy city, and setteth him on a pinnacle of the temple, And saith unto him, If thou be the Son of God, cast thyself down: for it is written, He shall give his angels charge concerning thee: and in their hands they shall bear thee up, lest at any time thou dash thy foot against a stone. Jesus said unto him, It is written again, Thou shalt not tempt the Lord thy God. Again, the devil taketh him up into an exceeding high mountain, and sheweth him all the kingdoms of the world, and the glory of them; And saith unto him, All these things will I give thee, if thou wilt fall down and worship me. Then saith Jesus unto him, Get thee hence, Satan: for it is written, Thou shalt worship the Lord

thy God, and him only shalt thou serve. Then the devil leaveth him,
and, behold, angels came and ministered unto him."

MATTHEW 4:1-10

Notice how Jesus was ready! He had the word on a hairpin trigger. He responded in strength against each attack of the devil. The devil is no match for the eternal word of God. It is an incorruptible seed. Once spoken, it releases God's power.

The devil tricks us into questioning our identity by saying, "If you're really the son of God, if you really are, then why don't you try it? Try to live right and be fatherhood, but it's not going to work. You've been a failure all your life. You might as well fail at this, too. Instead, why don't you just throw yourself into a bottle of alcohol? Throw yourself into drugs. Throw yourself down into depression and self-pity." If that doesn't work, he says, "If you just bow down and worship me, I'll let up on you. If you just bow down, I'll give you the promotion you want. It might be on Sundays, but I'll still give it to you." The devil will try to steal your affection from God! You control this. Don't let him.

Men, please heed these words! You're not by yourself. The Spirit of God is inside you. The anointing of God is inside you. You're not by yourself. When the devil tells you what you can't do, you tell him, "I can do it because it's not me; it's the Spirit of God inside of me." The Bible says the devil is the father of all lies (John 8:44). That must mean if he's telling you that you can't do it, he's scared that you're about to do it. If you're hearing what you can't do, step out. Tell the devil, "Since you said I couldn't do it…I know you're a liar…it must mean I can do it." The Spirit of God is inside you. The same God who raised Jesus from the dead is inside you. God is ready to resurrect some men into fatherhood. You're not by yourself. You're not alone. You're not defeated. It's not over.

You're not by yourself. You can do what you're reading. You can do it because it's not about what's on the outside; it's what's on the inside. The outside struggles are doing nothing more than confirming your ministry. The outside things are doing nothing more than confirming the anointing on the inside. It's time to take a stand. "I'm a man of God." If you want to retaliate against the devil, it's time to be transparent and take authority over every external struggle.

As men, we may struggle with all types of things: pornography, masturbation, drugs, illicit affairs, power, sexual identity and the list goes on. These are all traps of the devil to get you to accept that you are just a man. But now you are equipped to understand that you are not those things. You are a man of God with creative speaking power. You can cancel each of these things out of your life with the Word of God.

God established the male man with destiny inside him. We need to learn how to get a new respect for male men because they are the key to the success of everything. God establishes the male man, and then God turns around and gives him a wife. Everything is to flow out of this male man: stability, direction, guidance, protection, sustaining, maintaining, providing. When a male man has been fathered by God, he will stop the devil in his tracks! As long as the male man is intact, the devil can do very little.

When God gives the male man a wife, he is to protect her and cover her. He's standing guard. He's looking out for her best interests. Soon after, they have children. Now you have the male man, the female man and the offspring of their oneness. This is called a *family*. When individual families begin to dwell together, it's called a *community*. When you have groups of communities come together, it's called a *city*. Cities are groups of communities. Then when you have groups of cities come together, you have what's called a *nation*. Regardless of how big a nation becomes, it is still built on families. The nation's problems can all be solved if we focus on the family. We tend to try to deal with the problems at the higher level. If you want peace in the nation, it will come from peace in the home. As long as the church looks in the wrong place for a solution, the devil succeeds because we are distracted. We didn't have problems in the families until the foundation got knocked off. We didn't have problems with our wives or our children until the foundation got knocked off. Our communities were solid. What was knocked off? Fatherhood!

There was a time when cities were united and nations were united, but now what has happened is that satan has successfully gotten the man out of the way. Gotten him to leave his family or has put him behind bars. The devil has gotten the foundation of the family outside the home. Now that the fathers aren't there, the mothers are trying to lead and provide. Women are in an uncomfortable position that God never designed them to fill. A greater chasm is created between mothers and children. This leads to what has been called latchkey children. So, when the man was removed from the home, the woman was forced to fulfill a role she was not designed or intended to handle, which puts stress on the family. In fact, over 70% of black children are being raised in a house without a man. This is the devil's doing. We cannot correct what is wrong on the national level until we solve this basic fracture in the home.

Now fatherhood and motherhood are under assault, which leaves the children unprotected. Broken children will become broken adults without the intervention of God! This must be the focus of the church—to renew fatherhood at all costs. As long as the church stays emotional, men won't come back to the church because men are not emotionally made and can never truly identify in a purely emotional environment. If all men hear is an emotionally preached word that touches only their emotions and not their intellect, they will not fit in. They will consent to their wives and children attending church but the men will stay at home. Our church has taken this responsibility seriously and we have a greater percentage of men than most churches do because we are going to do our part to save the family by restoring the fatherhood ministry.

The church isn't focusing on the problem. The church is not focusing on the foundation. The church has been focusing on trying to build the church without first undergirding the foundation, the men. The church can truly go only as far as the men will take it. God wants both men and women to get in their proper place so His church and kingdom can be built and expanded. God wants fatherhood in position as the foundation so that the woman can get in her position. Her position is to be underneath her husband, underneath his covering and underneath his protection.

God never called for the woman to have to give direction. God never called for her to have to worry about how her family is going to pay the bills. God never called for her to have to deal with all these issues but with the absence of the male man, she had to step up. Now, don't get me wrong. The woman has stepped up very well. Frustrated but making it. Frustrated but dealing with it. However, because she has had to focus on a responsibility that was not intended for her to perform, she's very frustrated and very ineffective. Some churches have taken the easy route, which is to simply minister to whoever comes instead of solving the larger problem.

This pattern of men not being interested in church and their role in the church will continue to multiply until the church takes a stand and says, "We have an announcement. We are calling all men back into the house. We are calling men in. We're not calling you in to shout. We're not calling you in to jump. We're calling you in to celebrate who God created you to be." While the male man has been away, he's been smoking weed and sleeping around and doing all types of things, but it's because he doesn't know who he really is. He's thrown himself into all types of things to try and learn his identity.

You might have used drugs but it's not who you are. You might have gotten women pregnant out of wedlock but that's not who you are. I know some people have told you that you're a nobody, that you will amount to nothing, that you're never going to be anything and that you're just like your daddy. Most men don't know who they are but that's because nobody has stepped into their lives to tell them that that were made in God's image, that they are men of God and that the family cannot succeed without them.

I am calling on the Body of Christ to start a revolution by calling the men back to church. It may require that we change our worship styles and our preaching but if it gets more men to embrace their God-given role as fathers, it will be worth it. When the church begins to give a call to the men to resume their place, when the church is willing to take a stand and say that the men have a position they need to assume, when the church begins to say, "Calling all men, we need you to come back and lead us," and the men begin to respond and come back to their rightful place and take a covering position, something wonderful happens.

Boys are growing up without fathers in the house. It leaves a great void. Without the role model of a godly man, our boys are searching for identity in all the wrong things. However, when the father is restored to his rightful place, our boys will come back into alignment with God's will. The fathers are the ones who are the backbone. The fathers are the protectors. When the man is gone, the devil has a field day with the family. When the family is in order, its blessings and benefits cascade throughout society. Communities give birth to cities being in order. Cities give birth to nations being in order. When that happens, the Kingdom of God is in order. What I hope you are beginning to see is that it all ties back to the male man getting into his rightful place.

We have heard it said that, "You cannot judge a book by its cover!" We must stop judging men by their covers. Stop judging a man based on what he looks like. Stop judging a man based on how he's acting because if he's not acting in line with the Word, most likely he does not know. Instead of talking *about* him, talk *into* him. Remind him that he is created by God to lead. Remind him that he is the key to the salvation of the home. Remind him that the devil is afraid of him. Remind him that God is on his side.

If, as men, we take our rightful place, the devil will literally be abolished. Often, the problem with various men's conferences that draw large groups of men together is that the local churches that represent all those men drop the ball. After those men leave fired up, nobody in the local church is building on the experience they had at the conference. The men are left to themselves and that fire extinguishes. My heart is that this book will be a tool to help men walk out, on a daily basis, their purpose and destiny—especially as protectors.

CHAPTER 6

FATHERS
lead & teach

FATHERS,
lead & teach

The fourth function of fatherhood is *leader*. It is at this point that a man is ready for the responsibility of a wife because he is a life-giver, sustainer and protector. Having established that he can spend time with God and submit to God's fathering process, he's ready to learn how to lead others. If a man does not have a prayer life, he can't be a father because to be a father he must spend time with *the* Father.

Being the leader doesn't make a person better than anyone else. It simply means he's in a different position. The male man is the leader because he came first. God brought him forth first and gave him instructions for those following him. As the leader, it's the husband's responsibility to make sure his family remains on track concerning God's purpose and plan for them. Leadership is responsibility. In the Garden of Eden, God gave Adam the instructions concerning His standards. This is evident in the way God handled Adam and Eve's disobedience after they ate the fruit. God chastised Eve but confronted Adam about not obeying the instructions He had given him (Genesis 3:11). Some men read this and think God has empowered them to be tyrants within their homes but that could not be further from the truth. Being a man is not better than being a woman. Each gender has its own unique responsibility within the family structure but their value to God is equal. God holds the man responsible for maintaining and advancing the entire family according to His instructions found in the Bible.

> *"For the husband is the head of the wife,*
> *even as Christ is the head of the church:*
> *and he is the saviour of the body.*
> *Therefore as the church is subject unto Christ,*
> *so let the wives be to their own husbands in every thing.*
> *Husbands, love your wives, even as Christ also loved the church,*
> *and gave himself for it;"*

EPHESIANS 5:23-25

I don't want you to miss this. The leadership role of the man is a sacrificial role. It disturbs me when I see a man pervert his leadership role by dominating and terrorizing his family. The man should be willing to die for his family. If he is not, that man is not ready for marriage. Instead of asking, "Will you take this woman to be your wife?" maybe pastors should ask, "Are you prepared to lay down your life for the sake of your wife?" That clearly raises the bar!

In addition to the truth of the Bible, most women whom I have counseled state that they do not want to be in that leadership role. Often, because of the absence of men in the family, women have had to assume the responsibility in the home. This is commendable and we honor those women who stand strong with no male assistance. However, that is not God's best for the wife or the children. In some families, two or three generations of women have led the family because no men were present. This is the cycle that must be broken. It goes without saying that if the man is present in the home, he should be given the encouragement and support to lead. When the household is out of God's order, frustration arises. As I showed in the Introduction, almost every issue in society is traced back to the absence or inaction of a man.

The leadership role does not make the man infallible. In fact, the husband will most certainly make mistakes, as all leaders do. However, leadership identifies whom to hold accountable. When there are dysfunctions or problems within the family, "the buck" stops with the husband. Knowing that this mantle rests on the husband should cause each man contemplating marriage to seriously consider his maturity and readiness to lead his family in the ways of God. The man's leadership does not negate the woman's role in the family. I liken the interchange between the husband and the wife in the family to the Chief Executive Officer and the Chief Operating Officer in a corporation—neither can be successful without the other. A father leads.

The fifth function of fatherhood is *teacher*. The male man is supposed to be the teacher of the house.

> *"And, ye fathers, provoke not your children to wrath:*
> *but bring them up in the nurture and admonition of the Lord."*

EPHESIANS 6:4

The Bible directs this commandment to fathers and not mothers. God calls fathers to instruct their children and not to frustrate them. Fathers frustrate their offspring (and their wives) when they don't know their role and mismanage the authority God has placed in their hands. The Amplified Version of the Bible states that fathers should rear the children "tenderly." When fathers don't fulfill their role, children are negatively affected. It breeds anger within that child. You can see that anger present today in many children because they were not nurtured tenderly. The words are very intentional. "Bring them up" is the Greek word *ektrephō*, which means to "rear up to maturity." "Nurture" is from the Greek word *paideia* for "tutelage, education, or instruction." That word *nurture* means to mentor, and the word *mentor* means to tenderly train, to demonstrate, to teach, to counsel. In other words, nurturing is leading by example. "Admonition" is the Greek word *nouthesia*, which means "calling attention to, mild rebuke or warning." That word *admonition* in the Greek means "in balance." It means an equal balance of punishment and reward and correction and love. If you put it all together, this verse states, "Fathers, rear your children to maturity in the Lord through instruction and warning."

God has high expectations for the father! Instruction involves modeling the right behavior. The father can never call the family to do something he is not doing. Whether it is practicing spiritual disciplines or living with integrity, the entire family should look at the father as the role model. I have seen too many women bringing the children to church while the father is preoccupied with sports or just sitting at home. Inevitably, when that child, normally a little boy, becomes a teenager, he gravitates to the father's example and resists church attendance. It rings hollow when a father says, "You better go to church" and then stays at home. Dichotomous behavior like this has caused a generation to walk away from God.

The reason we have so many problems in the world today is because fathers aren't showing their children what to do. When one of my sons was five years old, he wanted to play organized football. I wasn't sending him on a field to be coached by somebody I didn't know. It just so happens that I enjoy football and am very knowledgeable about it. I didn't send my son, I went out on the field and was a coach. Often these coaches have good hearts, but their morality needs a lot of work. Their language and demeanor may not represent the highest standards. I wanted to be on the field coaching—having the experience with my son. I took time out of my schedule to coach. I didn't really want to coach but I didn't want to miss an opportunity to develop my son. Even if you are not knowledgeable in the area of your child's interest, attend as many practices as you can. Learn about the activity so that you can have intelligent conversations about it. Children are supposed to learn by what they see their father do. Men would do well to remember that eyes are always watching and learning and preparing to follow.

*"Train up a child in the way he should go:
and when he is old, he will not depart from it."*

PROVERBS 22:6

The word *train* comes from the Hebrew word *ḥânak* which literally means "to narrow"; figuratively, it means "to initiate or discipline." God's intention for discipline is that it has a purpose. Often
parents will discipline children from a place of anger and with no
purpose other than to inflict pain. Discipline implies instruction.
When a parent imposes discipline on a child, it should condition
him or her to avoid that behavior in the future. Discipline narrows
the options to the correct and accepted ones. Discipline, to be successful, must be consistent.

As parents, we start things but we don't keep them going. We
start good traditions in the home like family devotions and then, after a period of time, we get busy and stop them. This sends a mes-
sage to our children. We have not conditioned them to have daily
time with God; we have trained them to start things and not follow
through. Children observe inconsistencies. Fathers should be very
intentional about the behaviors they want to see in their children.
The discipline which that child receives reinforces those behaviors
and expectations. The time when the child becomes a teenager and
is ready to leave the house is too late. If you want the child to go
in the right direction, the father will need to consistently train that
child. Our children should be conditioned to spend time with God
daily through prayer and reading the Word to live a holy life, to serve
people, to attend church faithfully and the list goes on. Just like God,
you should start with the end in mind.

Determine what behaviors you expect in your children, then
take the time to train your children consistently so that those behaviors become a habit. In this regard, your children will not depart
from it when they are older. I have often heard this verse misquoted.

I hear people say, "Train up a child in the way that he should go and when he gets older he'll come back to it." This misstatement of Proverbs 22:6 shows what we fundamentally believe, which is that we expect the child to reject what he has been taught and then return at some later date. This is not God's plan. God wants every father to intentionally and consistently provide guidance and discipline to his children so that they continue to make good decisions and live for Him daily.

I was raised in a house that emphasized discipline. It was a non-negotiable requirement that we attend church every Sunday. If it was Sunday, it was time for church. When I prepared to go to college, I had already decided that I was not going to church. I miscalculated! It had become such a part of my routine that the Holy Spirit would not allow me to miss church—even at college. Sometimes I would be in church wondering why I was there. It had been instilled in me and I was not comfortable unless I was in someone's church on Sunday. Once you've done your best to discipline your children, trust that each seed sown will produce a harvest of obedience.

Another connotation of the word "train" is to connect to something, like how trains are connected to one another. There is always only one engine. The rest of the cars are along for the ride. When a father trains his children, he hooks them up to his leadership and carries them forward to their destiny. Those cars could never get to their destination without the engine pulling the way. A common mistake men make is to be the engine on one set of tracks but expect their children to be on another set of tracks without them. That system will not work because only the engine can pull a railroad car. If the child is on another track, he had no forward momentum. Fathers, you should understand that wherever you are leading, even if it is in the wrong direction, your children will follow. This incorrect worldly notion that a father's children should go further than him has polluted our understanding. The father leads the children to their destiny. Only when that father is no longer around do the children pick up the mantle and go further!

This is true with spiritual fatherhood as well. The children are carried forward by the spiritual father but the children are never better than he is. This type of thinking has put unbridled ambition in the hearts of our children and they are attempting to compete with their fathers. This is not the way God intended it. God intended for fathers to pull children to their destination; then, when those fathers transition to heaven, the children take the vision for the rest of the journey. Every man reading this must make an analysis. "Am I on the right track? What's my track saying? Are there pieces missing in my track? Is the track messed up? Does the track need repairs?" If it's not the track God put you on, your family can't switch until you switch. Once you switch, you bridge the gap for your family to switch. They can't switch on their own. They can't go, even though you won't go. They're stuck until you go. I believe that there are men who are reading this book and realizing that they have had their families on the wrong track. Once you make the move to get on the right track, the rest of the house will follow. They may be reluctant at first because they are unsure whether you will hold your course long term; however, just stay on the right track and they will follow you because fathers lead and teach.

CHAPTER 7

FATHERS CREATE
generations

FATHERS CREATE generations

Fathers are *progenitors*. This word that comes from Latin is composed of two words: Pro means "forth, before, in front of" and Genitor means "to beget." So, a progenitor is one who brings forth generations. The male man is called to be the start of generations. There is more to every male man than you know! You are ordained to produce generations. We see this displayed throughout the Old Testament. When God spoke to someone like Abraham, God addressed the generations within him.

> *"And in thy seed shall all the nations of the earth be blessed; because thou hast obeyed my voice."*

GENESIS 22:18

God has a long view of history and always has more in mind than simply the current generation. God told Abraham that his progeny would bless nations. This is why the Bible makes space to list who "begat" another. God wanted to show that what He does in one generation should carry forth in a greater measure in the next generation. From Adam all the way to you, God has more than you in mind. He wants you, as a man, to bring forth generations that will honor Him. This is a weighty responsibility and most men have never been told to prepare for generations.

Adam had the ability to determine the quality of life for his seed. Not just Adam but every man on this planet has the ability to affect either positively or negatively the quality of life of generations coming after him. Receive this word for your life! What a man does today is not affecting just him but also generations yet to come. The male man is the genesis of generations. He determines the quality of life of everybody coming out of him. We talked in a previous chapter about how families impact nations. This generational principle helps us understand how we arrived at the social condition we see around us today. It didn't happen overnight; instead, generation by generation, fathers moved away from God's principles. Everything comes back to the male man. Your grandfather did not realize that his conscious decision to walk away from the things of God put his son and grandsons in jeopardy. I firmly believe that if men realized this generational impact, they would operate differently today. A father brings people into being! Even though a man has a father, when he becomes a father he takes responsibility for creating new generations. God sees the entire family line but it is built from father to father to father. Your father may not have been everything he needed to be but now you are here. You can change and pass down blessings to the next generation. Whatever is in you will be passed down to the next generation. In the medical field, doctors screen for all types of conditions that may be in a family line. From a spiritual perspective, I am calling you to examine the type of spiritual life you are creating.

If you are living for God in your generation, you are preparing to bless the generations following you. We can look around today and see that we have fallen a long way from what previous generations called acceptable. You can look at television programs and see how what is permissible has changed, in a bad way. Let me explain how that happened.

One generation raised its children with strict guidelines and godly principles. That generation mandated church attendance and activity. Family life revolved around church. When that generation's children grew up, underestimating the importance of what they had been taught, they implemented new traditions. They felt that children should choose their own spiritual path without it being imposed upon them. By the time the third generation arose, there was no spiritual sensitivity and everyone did what they felt was right in their own eyes. This is the pattern that produced what we see today! The good news is that if you who are reading this book will reclaim generational responsibility, we can turn this trend around.

> *"And the Lord God formed man of the dust of the ground,*
> *and breathed into his nostrils the breath of life;*
> *and man became a living soul."*

GENESIS 2:7

God is a progenitor. What is inside of Him he deposits in his offspring (Adam). God breathed life into Adam and from that point Adam gave life to his generations. God determined the quality of Adam's life. The same is true of you. You are making a deposit into the next generation. You are positioning the next generation for either success or failure. When God breathed into Adam, God transferred His creative ability to Adam. Hebrew scholars note that man became a speaking spirit just like God. What's in you will go to the next generation.

That word *soul* means another speaking spirit like God. In other words, God put into Adam what was in Him, and that was the ability to do what He does. "You have the ability to do what I do, because I'm putting in you what's in me." I want you to see what God put into him because, again, a progenitor determines the quality of life of what comes out of him. Let's look at the quality of life God prepared for Adam. Go to Psalm 8:5. What quality of life did God determine for Adam?

> *"What is man, that thou art mindful of him? and the son of man,*
> *that thou visitest him? For thou hast made him a little lower than*
> *the angels, and hast crowned him with glory and honour. Thou*

madest him to have dominion over the works of thy hands; thou
hast put all things under his feet: All sheep and oxen, yea, and the
beasts of the field; The fowl of the air, and the fish of the sea, and
whatsoever passeth through the paths of the seas. O Lord our Lord,
how excellent is thy name in all the earth!"

PSALM 8:4-9

To truly understand the contextual impact of this statement, you must be aware of the translation fallacy in the text. A translation fallacy is when the translator, for whatever reason, die not translate the correct meaning of a word or sentence from the original Hebrew or Greek into English. If you look in the original Hebrew of this text, the word translated as *angels* is incorrect. The translator wrestled because the text actually has the word *Elohim*. *Elohim* means God. Thus, God made his creation as little versions of Himself. This may challenge some of your theological understandings, so let me give you more Biblical evidence.

"But to which of the angels said he at any time,
Sit on my right hand, until I make thine enemies thy footstool?
Are they not all ministering spirits,
sent forth to minister for them
who shall be heirs of salvation?"

HEBREWS 1:13-14

The Bible says that angels are sent to serve us. We are heirs of salvation. You cannot be over somebody you're serving. The angels are here to serve us, so we can't be a little lower than they are. Angels are here for you to command them. Angels are here to obey you. The contextual impact here is that God's quality of life for Adam was making him a little lower than God. If you are a little lower than God, the only thing above you is God. That means everything else is under you. Psalm 8 continues by saying that God gave us dominion! This is exciting because not only did God make us a little lower than He is, He gave us power over everything He created. Do you see how important you are to God? You operate under God's authority with His power. The creation story in Genesis demonstrates this.

"And Adam gave names to all cattle, and to the fowl of the air, and to every beast of the field; but for Adam there was not found an help meet for him."

GENESIS 2:20

God brought the animals to Adam to see what he would call them. Why would God do this? Because everything God created was given to Adam to manage. This is all in alignment with Psalm 8. The garden was a training ground for Adam to learn his potential and walk in his authority. I want to submit to you that the garden was the only suitable place where God would put him. If God had put him in any place lower than the garden, Adam would have been out of place because his quality of life had been determined at a high level, which came from God. When you come from royalty, you act royally. People who come from money act a certain way because they're used to a certain level. Unfortunately, many people don't know who they are, so they act beneath their created purpose. There's a quality of life that's in you that will not settle for anything less than the best.

Garden of Eden means "spot of heaven." God put Adam in a piece of heaven because heaven was the only thing good enough for him. God determined his quality of life. We learn from Genesis 3 that Adam lost this benefit because of sin. In response to Adam's sin, God determined a plan to restore humanity to its rightful place.

"For since by man came death, by man came also the resurrection of the dead. For as in Adam all die, even so in Christ shall all be made alive."

1 CORINTHIANS 15:22-23

"And so it is written, The first man Adam was made a living soul; the last Adam was made a quickening spirit."

1 CORINTHIANS 15:45

The Bible declares that Jesus was the last Adam because the one God was sending would be perfect. The one God sent would be without sin. The one God sent would get the job done. The first Adam fell because of disobedience, and it took him out of character. The second Adam reconnected because of obedience. The second Adam did the opposite of what the first Adam did. The second Adam said, "I'll be obedient unto death," and every step of obedience, every test of obedience, put him back into his character. In other words, the genes of God were flowing in him but it was his obedience that ultimately lined him up.

When Jesus restored humanity's character, it put everybody coming after him back in character. Many of us don't know we're back in character. Many of us are out of character. Many of you don't realize what's inside you, so you'll settle for things that are beneath you. You'll settle for just making it. You'll settle for just getting by. You'll settle for the devil's tricks. You'll settle for people talking about you, and you believe what they say.

You cannot believe the lies of the devil. You have the character of God in you. When Jesus came and was obedient, it brought me back to where I was before I was born in sin. Before you got here, do you know you existed? Your birthing was not your beginning. Your birthing was a manifestation of what you always were. Your birthing meant that there's something that came from the supernatural into the natural. Your birthing day was a supernatural experience for the world because something from heaven with the character of God was born into the planet. When you got here, you came in a supernatural way.

"Behold, I was shapen in iniquity;
and in sin did my mother conceive me."

PSALM 51:5

When you came out of your mother's womb you stepped into sin, and sin corrupted you. The real you was now covered up by a sin nature. The real you doesn't know what it is to fear. The real you doesn't know what it is to be depressed. The real you doesn't know what it is to back up and cower. The real you walks in complete courage, power and authority. The real you walks in complete obedience to the Father. The real you is not moved by what it sees. The real you walks in absolute faith. When you hit your mother's womb, you devolved into something that was not you, but God's confidence is in you becoming who He designed you to be.

God knows the tricks of the devil so He determined ahead of time to use every plan and scheme the devil concocts to draw you back to Him. God knew that those who lack character would bring pain and hurt to his children and God said that he would not let that destroy His people. This is God's strategy as generations face challenges. He uses them to draw the fathers back to Him.

"And we know that all things work together for good to them that
love God, to them who are the called according to his purpose."

ROMANS 8:28

There is no attack against God's progeny that He will not leave unanswered. Whatever the devil means for evil, God will turn it for good (Genesis 50:21). The power to overcome is available to you.

"And they overcame him by the blood of the Lamb, and by the word of their testimony; and they loved not their lives unto the death."

REVELATION 12:11

You can't have a *testimony* without a *test*. You can't have *come* through without *going* through. You can't be more than a conqueror without going through something that looks like it's going to conquer you. God gets you to Himself. You give your life to Him and now, after everything you went through, every aspect of something that was going to tear you down, you are armed with a weapon to give God glory. You went through *this* or *that*. You are now armed with something that you can use to go out in the world and search for somebody who looks just like you once did.

Religious people truly rub me the wrong way. Religion and religious people have messed up many people's lives. A religious person is ineffective in the Kingdom of God because they are a walking hypocrite who tries to portray perfection. A person walks in struggling with what the religious person "used to" struggle with, and the religious persons turns up their nose. It's only because of God's grace and mercy that the religious person is not struggling with that thing now. At the same time, we have some people in the church who lie. They walk around like they are free of stuff when they are actually still in it; they are in the closet with respect to it and don't want anybody to know they're still doing it. Some are singing on the platform and some are preaching on the platform and they are messed up in sin and not trying to come out. What the church must start teaching is that everybody has issues. Everybody has problems. Everybody has gone through stuff. Stop trying to cover it up. Instead, open your mouth and let somebody know, "This is what I went through," because somebody needs to hear what you have to say.

The male man has the ability to determine the quality of life for what comes out of him. This man puts his seed inside the woman and they birth a child. She gives birth to what's given to her. The power of a progenitor is not only that the man determines the quality of life of what first comes out of him, but the Bible says that he determines the quality of life of what comes out of him for generations. The power and anointing of a progenitor is what's harnessed and locked up inside the male man. He has the ability to affect not only his children but his children's children's children.

A generation is 40 years, and a man's lifespan is 120. From where he is, he can affect 120 years into the future. He can affect four generations. He can affect his current children and then his children's children's children.

"And it shall come to pass, if thou shalt hearken diligently unto the voice of the Lord thy God, to observe and to do all his commandments which I command thee this day, that the Lord thy God will set thee on high above all nations of the earth: and all these blessings shall come on thee, and overtake thee, if thou shalt hearken unto the voice of the Lord thy God."

DEUTERONOMY 28:1-2

If you are a father (or a father-to-be), now is the time to align yourself with God so that you are prepared to pass down a spiritual blessing to your progeny. When you have children, you'll have no problem doing the Word. As fathers or fathers-to-be, how we reverse the curse is obedience. According to what we just read, obedience causes blessings to overtake you. Obedience causes blessings to overtake your children and your children's children and your children's children's children. Obedience is what reverses the curse. My wife and I made up our minds a long time ago that we would pass down only spiritual blessings to our progeny. Our families were a mess: a bunch of trifling men. Nobody wanted to live for God. Everybody wanted to do their own thing. Everybody wanted to get high, get drunk, beat up women and not work. God will always have somebody who will stand up and say, "Enough of that." My wife and I came together and I said, "Listen. You have mess in your family. I have mess in my family. Drugs are in your family. Drugs are in my family. All types of sexual immortality are in your family, and it's the same in my family. Abuse is in your family; it's in my family. I think we ought to take a stand and say, 'Enough is enough.'"

Before we had kids, I said, "We have to work on our children and our children's children and our children's children's children so that if God tarries, when we're dead and gone, we were the catalyst for change in our family." We began to declare to God, "Father, we are going to serve you all the days of our lives." With our words and actions lining up with God and His Word, we began to intentionally shoot things into the future to hit our children, grandchildren and great-grandchildren. We decided to line up so we could shoot prosperity and not poverty into the future to our seed four generations away. We have grandchildren and great-grandchildren depending on us to create a future that is conducive for them to succeed.

If Jesus doesn't come until after I'm gone, somewhere along the line great-grandchildren can turn back and say, "When we look back at the Edmondson household, there was all this mess back there. Nobody could stay married back there. Drugs back there. Husbands beating up their wives back there. Wives wouldn't line up in submission back there. All this mess back there. But at this point in our family lineage, everything seemed to turn because somebody made a commitment to change what they did to prepare the way for those coming behind them."

When you disregard the generations coming after you, you are continually shooting curses into the future; those curses are going after your seed and hitting your seed. You can't look at the misbehavior of your seed and wonder where that behavior came from. It started in the previous generation. Today you can make a quality decision to change the generations within you. You are a speaking spirit who can command change. Please understand that your words must also line up with your lifestyle.

As you begin to speak, blessings go after your seed and overtake them! The blessing takes your seed to their Promised Land. You can't go in the future in the natural, but in the spirit you can talk to your seed. Speak generational blessings over yourself, your seed and future generations. Curses will be broken and the blessing of God will overtake your seed.

"And if thou wilt walk before me, as David thy father walked, in integrity of heart, and in uprightness, to do according to all that I have commanded thee, and wilt keep my statutes and my judgments: Then I will establish the throne of thy kingdom upon Israel for ever, as I promised to David thy father, saying, There shall not fail thee a man upon the throne of Israel."

1 KINGS 9:4-5

God honors generations. God told Solomon that he would be blessed if he walked in the same manner as his father, David. David was not perfect but he had a heart toward God. He passed down a blessing to Solomon. Solomon was successful because of David. God knows that you have faults but you don't have to pass them down.

"…he raised up unto them David to be their king; to whom also he gave testimony, and said, I have found David the son of Jesse, a man after mine own heart, which shall fulfil all my will. Of this man's seed hath God according to his promise raised unto Israel a Saviour, Jesus:"

ACTS 13:22-23

Jesus was from David's blessed progeny. What I am saying to every man reading this is that wherever you are, whatever you've done, whatever you've said, if you want to correct it right now, today, repent with a sincere heart. Say something like this: "God, I've been messing up. I've been running astray. I want to be licensed and authorized to stop sending curses down to my seed and begin to send blessing to my seed's seed's seed."

It starts with you. It's not about what you've done. It's not about what you've said. It's not about what you haven't done. It's about recognizing today the faults you have and, instead of justifying, instead of debating, simply repenting. The Bible says if you repent with a sincere heart, God is faithful and just to forgive you of your sins and cleanse you from all unrighteousness (1 John 1:9). Repentance allows you to move forward. Then the blessing will surround you and overtake you. The blessing leads you around the curses of your forefathers and takes you to your blessed place. The blessed place represents all your dreams, aspirations and visions.

Men, we must connect with our Heavenly Father because we have generations counting on us to act properly and speak blessings! As you live that Word, regardless of what you see, regardless of what you hear, regardless of what you've been through, regardless of what you've done, you are now pushing your blessing to seed that you might never see.

CHAPTER 8

FATHERS UPHOLD

FATHERS UPHOLD

The eighth function of fatherhood is *upholder*. To be an *upholder* means "to bear or to carry." Fatherhood is about more than producing children. This is to single men, to men without children who are married, and to men who have children. The father is the one who is called by God to carry that family on his back. Every man is anointed to do that. There are burdens that come with being the head of a home and you need to be ready to assume them. There is a heavy weight associated with being God's man in the home. Sometimes there are heavy things we carry but there is a redemptive purpose. It can be likened to when Jesus carried the cross on his back to Golgotha.

Jesus bore all of humanity's sins on that cross but there was a higher purpose, which was the salvation of mankind. I am not suggesting that any other human can do what Jesus did. However, there are things that we, as fathers, are called to bear on behalf of our families. When we say, "I do" to a wife, we are saying, "I will" to bearing all the challenges related to being in the family.

The father is the foundation of every family. Foundations are vital to any strong building. If the foundation is weak, a beautiful structure may be built upon it but it won't stand for long. A good builder makes sure the foundation is built well because the safety and soundness of the structure depend upon it. Now I want to show you how God is an upholder and that this function of fatherhood flows down from Him to us as fathers in the earth.

"God, who at sundry times and in divers manners spake in time past unto the fathers by the prophets, Hath in these last days spoken unto us by his Son, whom he hath appointed heir of all things, by whom also he made the worlds."

HEBREWS 1:1-2

God used to speak to the fathers through the prophets. Now He speaks to the fathers through the Son, who is Jesus Christ the Living Word of God. If you want to know about fatherhood, if you want to learn how to live as a father, you must look in the Word. Jesus is the expressed image, or manifested image, of his Father. If you want to know what God looks like, just look at Jesus. If you want to know how God acts, look at Jesus. Jesus is the expressed, manifested image of God.

Here's the first question. Where did that develop? We know that Jesus was a man. But He was also God. It didn't just happen that way. It had to develop. Where did it develop? Where did Jesus's image develop? It developed in the time he spent with the Father in prayer and obeying the Father's instructions. Jesus said, *"I only say and do what I see the Father say and do"* (John 5:19). Jesus spent time with the Father. Men, we must spend time with God. I must spend time with God to express Him to my family. In other words, you can't live for God and express God to your family if you're not spending time with Him and obeying what He says. If you are not spending time with God as a man, you are creating a deficit. As an expression of fatherhood in the earth, you must spend time with God learning how God operates. As men, we should be doing nothing more than expressing what God is telling us in our time with Him. You cannot read the Bible and not have a relationship with the Author of the Bible. If you read the Bible but don't have a relationship with the Author, you will lack the proper understanding. You need time with the Author, which will give you revelation of what the Author is saying to you. Let's look at the Hebrews passage and see what we discover about this fatherhood function of upholder that flows from God to us.

"Who being the brightness of his glory, and the express image of his person, and upholding all things by the word of his power, when he had by himself purged our sins, sat down on the right hand of the Majesty on high."

HEBREWS 1:3

God upholds all things through His Word. God upholds each person through His Word. Every born-again believer should have some Word from God that he or she holds onto in order to deal with whatever situation arises. How many things is *all things*? Is there anything excluded from *all things*? God's Word upholds all things, so that means for everything I'm dealing with that's trying to fall down around me, God's Word is meant to uphold it. God's Word will hold you and your family when forces are trying to pull you down. In whatever endeavor you undertake, found it on the Word of God if you desire success.

If you want to start a business, what Scripture upholds you when obstacles appear? Whenever you feel the pressure of the business, the first words from your mouth should be Scripture. No one else's word has the power to change your situation. One Word from God will keep you in the most violent storm. This goes beyond emotion! God needs his men well-grounded in the Word so they can stand and, if necessary, uphold the family through the storms of life.

It is hard being a man in today's society. It is harder being a father. What makes you successful is God's Word. His Word will hold you and your family. The men who aren't upholding their families right now are the men who don't have the Word in them like they should.

When a man has the Word in him, regardless of what happens, he will stand firm in supporting his family. When something comes against my family, even if it's not my fault, I will bear the weight of it because I know that as God holds me, He will hold my family. I carry the load for my family's actions. When you became one with your wife, you committed to uphold her. She is a part of you. Regardless of who makes mistakes, the man takes responsibility for the actions of the family because they are all a part of his generations.

When Adam and Eve sinned, God could have left them to fend for themselves. However, He knew they were His creation and needed restoration. God put a plan in place to uphold them until a way could be made for them to return to Him.

"And I will put enmity between thee and the woman,
and between thy seed and her seed; it shall bruise thy head,
and thou shalt bruise his heel."

GENESIS 3:15

God took responsibility for Adam's actions but He didn't take blame for Adam's actions. Taking responsibility does not mean taking blame. A father will reconcile whoever has make mistakes in the family. I'm not talking about you assigning something to be done or you delegating something for your family to take care of and it doesn't get done. Yes, you are responsible but you still must discipline the situation. If you have your children do something and they don't do it, you don't walk in and say, "I'm to blame." No, no, I'm not to blame. I didn't mess up. But I take responsibility for it not getting done. If you have delegated your wife to do something, if you two have discussed things and she agreed that she was going to handle something and you agreed that you were going to handle something else and she doesn't get it done, you now must talk to your wife. You don't just say, "That's on you," because it's not. You're the head. You're still responsible, so you must confront and talk and communicate and make sure things get done.

An upholder will take responsibility for the actions of his family. I want to show you this awesome point in the Word of God.

"Forasmuch as ye know that ye were not redeemed with corruptible things, as silver and gold, from your vain conversation received by tradition from your fathers; but with the precious blood of Christ, as of a lamb without blemish and without spot: who verily was foreordained before the foundation of the world, but was manifest in these last times for you…"

1 PETER 1:18

God took care of your sin before you ever sinned. This verse says that Jesus was foreordained to redeem humanity. God takes such responsibility for the actions of His children and that is why He took care of our sins. There are still consequences resulting from your sin, and God disciplines you because of your sin, but He takes the responsibility for your sin to get you free of it.

That should be liberating because God had a make-up for your mess-up before your mess-up ever existed. If you're walking around saying, "Does God love me? I don't know if He'll love me anymore because of this, that or the other," you need to understand that God loves you so much. Nothing can separate you from God's Love.

"What shall we then say to these things? If God be for us, who can be against us? He that spared not his own Son, but delivered him up for us all, how shall he not with him also freely give us all things? Who shall lay any thing to the charge of God's elect? It is God that justifieth. Who is he that condemneth? It is Christ that died, yea rather, that is risen again, who is even at the right hand of God, who also maketh intercession for us. Who shall separate us from the love of Christ? shall tribulation, or distress, or persecution, or famine, or nakedness, or peril, or sword? As it is written, For thy sake we are killed all the day long; we are accounted as sheep for the slaughter. Nay, in all these things we are more than conquerors

through him that loved us. For I am persuaded, that neither death, nor life, nor angels, nor principalities, nor powers, nor things present, nor things to come, Nor height, nor depth, nor any other creature, shall be able to separate us from the love of God, which is in Christ Jesus our Lord."

ROMANS 8:31-39

This is why God doesn't cut us off when we make mistakes. He loves us! You, as a father, must possess this same unconditional love for your family. Being an upholder is an attitude. It's an attitude driven by unconditional love that calls you to uplift your family in spite of the bad things they've done. The head of the home is responsible for everything that happens in his family. Even if I work more than my wife does, even if I'm busier, I am responsible. When you embrace being an upholder, you don't push blame; you push solutions. If you will accept responsibility for the actions of your family, the devil has no place. He has place only when a man will refuse to accept responsibility. In other words, if the devil is in your family, it is because the man has given him place. You might be saying, "How am I going to do that? How am I going to take responsibility for everything in my family even when I didn't do anything wrong? It's hard just keeping myself together. It's hard just trying to make sure I am doing things right." Well, if you want to be an upholder, don't try to do it yourself. My objective here is to get you to stop trying alone. If you try on your own, you will not succeed. You must stop trying. You must adopt Jesus' approach. Jesus came to earth as the Son of God. However, He was not free to do whatever he wanted to do.

"I can of mine own self do nothing: as I hear, I judge: and my judgment is just; because I seek not mine own will, but the will of the Father which hath sent me."

JOHN 5:30

Jesus, as the Savior of the world, limited himself to doing only what his Father instructed. Jesus was not left on his own to accomplish the task. Jesus was upheld by the Father and was protected by the Father.

In a similar manner, The Heavenly Father upholds Jesus and Jesus upholds the man and the man uphold the family. If Jesus didn't try to do anything on his own, within his own strength, why in the world should we try to? Look at how Paul states this.

"But I would have you know, that the head of
every man is Christ; and the head of the woman is the man;
and the head of Christ is God."

1 CORINTHIANS 11:3

So, you see that headship is not about power or control; it is about bearing the burden for another. It is a sad day when a man tries to shoulder the challenges of the family in his own strength. It will leave him exhausted. Also, we have the example of satan, who made a decision that he didn't want to be upheld anymore. The rebellion that satan staged was his way of telling God, "I don't need you anymore." Everything that satan touches crumbles because he is not upheld by God.

Men, you must understand that, as the upholder, you can fulfill your duty only when Jesus, the Living Word, upholds you. Any time you step away from God and His Word for any reason, your family is not being upheld. At that point, your life and family will crumble because, in the words of Jesus, "of your own self you can do nothing."

Now I want to address an obvious concern that a single mother may have when reading this. What is she to do when the man who was supposed to uphold the family walks away? That's a great question. Ultimately God upholds your family, so you are still covered. It is not His perfect plan but He will not leave you uncovered. God will uphold you. He will give you the strength and the grace to keep going so that your purpose is not derailed by the man's bad decision. You don't have to be concerned that you are a target for the devil because the devil cannot defeat a child of God. The devil can't just come in and take the family—and there's a specific reason why he can't. God said, *"He suffered no man to do them wrong: yea, he reproved kings for their sakes; Saying, Touch not mine anointed and do my prophets no harm"* (Psalm 105:14-15). That doesn't mean exclusively preachers. In the Old Testament, the anointed ones were the prophets; however, now, if you read your Bible, you can see that *you're* anointed because the Anointed One is inside you. The devil can't just run all over that family because there is still an anointed woman of God on the scene and the devil can't touch God's anointed.

The devil can't touch the woman but what he *can* do is say things to her to make her feel as though she's going to crumble. "You're not going to make it. Nobody wants you. You have no income. You have no education. What are you going to do? You're *this*. You're *that*. Nobody likes you. That's why that man left you already. Nobody else is going to come to you. You're going to be stuck in this rut all the days of your life. Got you! And your seed, too." When the devil puts pressure on you like this, his sole purpose is to get you to open your mouth and speak words of death. Remember: *"Death and life are in the power of the tongue: and they that love it shall eat the fruit thereof"* (Proverbs 18:21). If the devil can get the woman to speak negative words about her situation, she empowers the situation to overtake her with her verbal permission. The reality, though, is that her situation, regardless of what it appears to be, doesn't have to overtake her and the family. Even though the man has left what appears to be a gap, God has made provision for the gap to be filled.

Have you ever wondered why, when the father leaves, a single mom is able to overcome all the problems she must confront? I come from a single-parent home because the father left. It seemed like the whole world was going to cave in. My mother was dealing with financial issues. She was struggling with children issues and school issues. She had to handle it all by herself. How does a mom overcome when things are going on like that in the father's absence? It's because of something called *grace*. What is grace? *Grace* is the empowering presence of God that helps you be what you need to be so you can do what you're called to do and have what you're called to have. In other words, grace helps this mom rise up under the things that are happening and be the head of the household. Even though she's not called to it, even though she's not supposed to do it, grace allows her to rise up and be the head and the anointed one. She has the empowering presence of God; she can lead her family so the family can have the blessings of God and not wallow in the absence of the man even though she may miss him.

The single mother who is a believer has the Holy Spirit guiding and directing her. The Holy Spirit will give her wisdom to navigate all the situations around her. The single mother has *goodness* and *mercy* trailing her, according to Psalm 23:6. One of the translations of the word *goodness*, amongst about eight of them, is "economic wisdom." That's good news! God gives economic wisdom to those over whom He is Shepherd so that they can thrive in all seasons. Then the single mother has mercy. One of the meanings of *mercy* is favor. Favor is God raising up others to use their power, ability and influence to help me. That woman and family who were left to fend for themselves have goodness (economic wisdom) and mercy (favor) following them everywhere they go.

Even with this understanding, the mom who's in this position may be very negative by focusing on who left her instead of who is currently with her. Her mentality may be, "I don't want to go through this. I can't believe he left me. God, where are you now? I need you. Where are you? I can't believe this. I don't want to be in this situation. I can't stand it." Talking negatively because of frustration will only make the situation worse. If she will listen, the Holy Spirit will convince her of what is around her. The Holy Spirit will say, "Listen. I'm here with you. Goodness and mercy are behind you. Grace is on top of you. You can make it. You're not by yourself." To the single mother reading this, that is the word I remind you of again: You're not by yourself. You're not alone. Stop talking negatively because God has called you, just like Abraham, to speak those things that be not as though they are (Romans 4:17). God has called you to stand strong. God has called you to stand still. Don't talk negatively. You can do it. You can make it. It is not over. You can and will win if you let grace, goodness and mercy work for you.

"I am crucified with Christ: nevertheless I live; yet not I, but Christ liveth in me: and the life which I now live in the flesh I live by the faith of the Son of God, who loved me, and gave himself for me. I do not frustrate the grace of God: for if righteousness come by the law, then Christ is dead in vain."

GALATIANS 2:20-21

Without grace, nothing in God's kingdom works. Faith and grace work hand in hand. If you don't allow grace to do its job, nothing in God's kingdom will work. Therefore, you can believe God by confessing and standing on Scripture. However, if you're trying to do anything yourself, grace can't work for you. Grace was called to help you be what you couldn't be on your own. If you are trying to do it, grace will be frustrated. Does it say live by your talents? Faith in your giftings? Faith in your education? We are supposed to live by the faith of the Son of God.

There's a colon in the actual text because it's referring to the prior statement. The prior statement is that if you *live* instead of Christ *living in you*, you will frustrate the grace of God. If you try to live by what you know and by what you can do, you frustrate the grace of God. The moment you try to do things within the confines of your own strength, you cancel the grace of God. Grace is called to empower you to do what you can't. Nothing in the Kingdom of God can be accomplished by human effort alone. Grace must work with you and for you. If you don't collaborate and cooperate with grace, you frustrate God's grace.

The grace of God fills the gap left by the man! Grace will uphold and sustain the woman. If God brings back that man, the grace doesn't leave! It still helps support that family but now the house is back in order because the man has come to his senses and assumed his place. Gentlemen, when you are back in position you forfeited, allow the grace that caused your wife to hold things down while you were gone work for you, too. If you try to do things only within your own strength, you will not uphold anything; rather, you will barely survive. Over time, the weight of life against you as the upholder will overwhelm you. Grace will shout, "Will you stop trying?" Grace says, "I'll go do it." Grace says, "I'll make it work because I'm here to do what you cannot do by yourself." You can't be an upholder of your family by your might or your strength but only by His spirit (Zechariah 4:6). It is the grace of God in your life that causes you to uphold those around you.

If you're a man reading this and you're frustrated, know that your frustration is tied directly to grace being frustrated in your life. While you're trying to do it in your own strength, grace is hindered. Grace is your power to flow, but grace can't flow until you go. Grace can't flow until you get out of the way. Stop being confident in yourself. Stop being confident in what you can do. You can't do anything by yourself. It's not about you. Go to God and receive His grace. A frustrated man is a non-praying man because if you spend time with God, God will tell you exactly what to do, exactly what to think and exactly where to go. Grace will do that which you cannot do. Stop trying to achieve on your own. You are going to fail. You are going to hurt yourself. You are not going to succeed because you weren't called to try but to trust. You're called to stand and be the upholder of your family by the grace of God.

Open your mouth and speak. Cover your family. Stand strong. The Word of God upholds you. God called you to stand firm in faith, relying on His grace. When you stand and you speak, grace flows on the words you spoke. When you speak, finances will line themselves up. When your family is sick, don't go running in panic and fear.

Be the upholder and speak healing into your family. Stop looking to your pastor and church for a breakthrough in your family. Your pastor is not anointed to get your wife's breakthrough. *You're* anointed for it; the grace is on you.

Quitting is not an option. Men of God don't quit. We might get knocked down but we get back up. We might wobble but we don't fall. Quitting is not in you. You can't quit.

All my life, people have told me, John Edmondson, what I could not do. All my life I've heard, "You can't go to college because you come from a single-parent family. You can't do *this*. You can't do *that*." I've had to fight for everything. I refused to be denied. I refused to quit. I want all that God has for me and my family and the generations coming behind me.

You can't quit, gentlemen. You must cover your family. "Well, I'm not married." You're covering your future wife and children. You cannot quit. If you fail, get up. I know what it's like to fail. I've been there. Failure is success turned inside out. You will never succeed if you don't fail. You must fail first so you can handle success. If you fail, get up. You must stand for your families, both present and those family members coming behind you.

At the heart of this book is the desire to get men to rise up and assume their rightful place in God's plan for the family. I want to stir you to trust God more so that your family walks in all of God's blessings. We're standing for our families. We're standing because we're fathers. Fathers, don't quit. Fathers, after having done all to stand, stand some more by the grace of God. Keep standing, men.

CHAPTER 9

FATHERS CULTIVATE

FATHERS CULTIVATE

The tenth and final function of fatherhood is a *cultivator*. A cultivator develops and makes things better. Gentlemen, concerning your spouse and your children, God has assigned you to develop them and make them better each and every day. When God blesses a man, God has an expectation that the man will enhance that which has been placed in his hands. Men are stewards. A steward is a manager. Men do not own their families; God does. Thus, a man must operate with his family according to God's instructions. God's charge to the man is to improve that which has been placed under his management.

When God gives you a wife, He expects that you will be a force for good in her life by helping her grow up and become the woman God created her to be. When a man and woman get married, neither of them is all that God has called them to be. As God develops the man, the man encourages, supports and helps his wife fulfill her destiny. The same is true when the children arrive. God's plan is for the father to cultivate those children into Kingdom assets.

I hear men complain all the time about the deficits they identify in their wives. They have a detailed list of things they don't like. However, those men are missing their calling. Men are ordained to cultivate their spouses to be who God created them to be. This will cause your wife to be the woman of your dreams! You will never get tired of the woman of your dreams. You enjoy spending time with the woman of your dreams.

There has been a repeated word throughout all these fatherhood functions, and it's the word "responsibility." When the man views his role as a cultivator, it comes with a responsibility—a grave one. The husband can discover God's plan for his wife only by spending time with God and spending time with his wife. God wants to share his heart's desire for His daughter. Also, you should hear your wife share her heart about all she believes God wants her to do. It is with these two inputs (from God and from his wife) that the man can ask the Holy Spirit to show him how to assist his wife in growing to be who she knows God wants her to be. You can only imagine how difficult this process would be when either the man or the woman does not know Jesus. The Bible's admonition remains true:

"Be ye not unequally yoked together with unbelievers:
for what fellowship hath righteousness with unrighteousness?
and what communion hath light with darkness?"

2 CORINTHIANS 6:14

A cultivator facilitates the fulfillment of another person's dreams. If your wife has dreams to accomplish certain tasks, your goal is to serve her in her pursuit. Marriage is not all about the man, with everyone else serving his needs. Quite to the contrary, God has purpose and destiny on every member in the family. No one person can be all he or she is called to be unless the others in the family are doing what they are called to do. This interconnectedness neutralizes selfishness on the man's part. A cultivator will not be intimidated by his wife's or children's dreams. In fact, he should be inspired because all this is a part of God's plan that was formed from the beginning of time.

Help develop your wife and children. If there are classes, certifications or contacts needed, cultivate them. There may be callings on your wife's life that she is too timid to pursue. You should not just let her leave that area undeveloped. Cast vision and encourage her to obey God and support her unconditionally.

I have always known that my wife had a calling to preach but she did not embrace it. As far as preaching, she would rather sit on discussion panels with others. However, it was my job to cultivate her to be what she's called to be. I didn't force her but I did encourage her. I continually reminded her that she had an awesome calling on her life. Early on, when she would get up to minister, even if she didn't do as well as she wanted to, I was the first to encourage her. I did not put her down or criticize her, as she was taking a first step toward her destiny. I kept encouraging her, developing her and cultivating her. Soon she began to blossom and flourish as a preacher in her own right.

Since those early days, she has grown into a seasoned minister of the gospel who has preached on all types of platforms and blessed so many people with her ministry gifts. She's become very confident in who she is, and is extremely sensitive to the Spirit of God. Why? Because I kept reassuring her with statements like, "You're an awesome woman of God."

"Who can find a virtuous woman?
for her price is far above rubies."

PROVERBS 31:10

This is a serious question. Many men are looking for the virtuous woman rather than cultivating the virtuous woman. You're not going to find her because you're looking in the wrong place. God will tell you what you need to do to develop your wife. The fact of the matter is, you may not be spending time with Him so that He can talk to you. My wife is my focus. I desire with all my heart to see her living every dream God has put in her heart. I get excited when she shares new aspects of what she believes God is calling her to do. I am never threatened by her dreams because I know God has anointed me to cultivate her so that she will accomplish His dreams.

One of the greatest assets in the process is time. When men pursue women before marriage, they are willing to spend as much time as possible to "catch their prey." However, once the woman becomes his wife, the man minimizes the amount of time he spends digging deeper into who she is and what her passions are. Prior to getting married, I pursued my wife. I mean, I pursued her and hunted her down. She went to college to get an education; I went to college to get her. That's what I majored in: Isha Maria Green. I came up with creative ideas for romancing her and enticing her—creative stuff just to let her know how special she was to me.

Quite honestly, when we got married I stopped the pursuit. The problem is, the devil tries to pervert what God intends. Most times, as men, we stop the pursuit when we step over the threshold. Having been married for over 25 years, I shout loudly to you: "Don't stop the pursuit!"

> *"Husbands, love your wives, even as Christ also*
> *loved the church, and gave himself for it;"*

EPHESIANS 5:25

It does not say, "Compare her to another woman." It says, "Husbands, love your wives." Don't tell her, "I wish you were like so-and-so. I wish you would be like the pastor's wife." You don't really know the pastor's wife. You might discover that your wife was better off than you thought. The chief responsibility of the husband is to love the wife. If you love your wife, criticism won't dominate your conversation. If you love your wife, you will be committed to her cultivation. If you love your wife, you will celebrate every milestone along the journey to be all God created her to be. I always say: "Nobody has the anointing for my wife. There's a special anointing that comes with her." You must be strong. You must be focused. No weak, spineless man could handle my wife because she will break you down. But I have the anointing, the burden-removing, yoke-destroying anointing needed to handle Mrs. Isha M. Edmondson.

Don't compare your wife to another woman. If you're comparing her, you're not cultivating her; you're tearing her down. If she lacks anything, which she will, just like you will, develop her. Don't put anything above this fatherhood function, even if you are in ministry. Be careful not to confuse your priorities. Ministry cannot be first! Your wife must be first. Don't put the church above your wife. Don't spend all your time working on *His* project and very little time on *your* wife. If you spend very little time on *your* wife, you disqualify yourself from working on *His* project. Old-school ministers used to say, "It's my relationship with God first, then my relationship with the church, then my relationship with the wife." This unscriptural thinking is the heart of why so many ministry families struggle. The wrong priorities keep everyone outside the will of God. Love *your* wife by focusing on cultivating her.

> *"That he might sanctify and cleanse it with the washing of water by the word."*

EPHESIANS 5:26

Husbands/fathers, speak the Word over your wife. Speak to her dreams. Speak to her destiny. Speak forth gifts, callings, abilities and new levels of operating. Don't speak your opinion. Don't speak your frustration. Don't speak your disappointment. Speak the Word. She is never going to be what she was called to be if you don't keep your mouth in alignment with God's Word for her. Don't speak *at* her; speak *over* her.

Paul said, "Love your wife like Jesus loves the church. Do for your wife like Jesus does for the church." Personally, I continually work on putting my wife first. I love the church that my wife and I founded but my wife is first. I will not take the platform in my church and preach if my family is out of order. If I don't have the anointing to keep my family straight, what anointing do I have to preach the Word in that moment?

My family is my priority before ministry. My wife is before my kids. I love my three boys, Joshua, Christian and Jordan, with all my heart. They are my people but my wife is first in my life because I'm commanded to love her the way Christ loved the church, and Christ was willing to die for the church. Jesus died for the church so that I don't have to. The Bible makes it clear that the married person must make his spouse a priority.

"But I would have you without carefulness. He that is unmarried careth for the things that belong to the Lord, how he may please the Lord: but he that is married careth for the things that are of the world, how he may please his wife."

I CORINTHIANS 7:32

For the husband, the wife must be a priority above all else. This is modeled after Jesus's example. The church, with all its blemishes, remains Jesus's top priority. He is cultivating the church to be everything He destined her to be.

"...that he [Jesus] might present it to himself a glorious church, not having spot, or wrinkle, or any such thing; but that it should be holy and without blemish."

EPHESIANS 5:27

Jesus lovingly develops the church to be his glorious bride without any defects. In a similar manner, a husband should lovingly care for his wife and nurture her so she strengthens the weak areas and becomes the woman God created her to be. If there are deficits in the relationship, a cultivator will collaborate with the wife to create a plan for growth and development.

Glory is the reflection of a thing. The church becomes glorious when it looks like Jesus. Husbands who cultivate their families end up with families that resemble the order of God. I cannot stress this enough. The husband must spend time with God to understand God's heart for the man's wife. Once the man has this vision in his heart, he can help cultivate his wife into the image of her Heavenly Father. In a practical sense, a wife will be a reflection of her husband. Today, I look at my wife and I marvel at the wife, mother and pastor she has become. I am proud to see her flow in her multiple callings because I know that she represents the result of the cultivation God has done through me. I have seen other pastor's wives who look repressed and oppressed. Their eyes are sad and you can tell that there is an unfulfilled vision and destiny in their lives. That woman's sadness is directly attributable to the cultivation of the husband. No pastor should ever be happy with a flourishing ministry and a floundering marriage.

I want you to get this, single men. If God has called you to be married, you're called to be a cultivator. Therefore, a woman who comes into your presence should leave cultivated, not pregnant. She shouldn't be taken advantage of. When a woman comes into your presence, single men, she should leave one of three ways.

First, she should leave *blessed*. When she is with you, she should have a good, positive fellowship experience. I always recommend that this be in a public place to lessen temptation. You should have a good time together. Second, she should leave *edified*. To edify means to build up. A man ready to be a husband and father will build up the woman in his life. In essence, she should feel better because she was in your presence. This is not limited to the woman to whom you have a romantic attraction. Any person who leaves the presence of a man walking in the fatherhood ministry will be edified.

The third way she should leave your presence is *challenged*. A male man who has been properly fathered will inspire those around him to stretch to be more. If the person you meet is not a believer, she should feel a sense of conviction to pursue God. If the person has a mindset that is self-defeating, after she has encountered a God-led man, she will question her attitudes and behaviors and make changes. If she is a believer, she should leave the man with a yearning to be more for God. I know that as you are reading this it seems unrealistic. How can being in the presence of a man cause all this to happen? Well, it's simple! If a man spends enough time in God's presence, God will rub off on him. We call this the anointing. All men should desire this level of functioning because it means lives will not be the same.

Single ladies, please get this. If a man does not know how to cultivate you, it means he is not spending time with God. If he doesn't know how to be a cultivator, he knows only how to destroy. Please pause to receive this! A man will either cultivate or destroy. A cultivator develops or makes better. Somebody who does not understand cultivating will do the direct opposite of cultivating. Instead of developing and making better, they will make worse or destroy.

As a pastor, I regard every woman in my church as one of my daughters. I am very protective of their singlehood. My wife spends a great deal of time with the women, as do I, so we can teach them to reject counterfeit men. Those single daughters have been assigned to me. I do not compromise in that area. If a man doesn't know how to cultivate, he will destroy you. If he doesn't know how to cultivate, he will destroy the children. If he doesn't know how to cultivate, he'll destroy his career.

If a man comes into your presence, single ladies, do not ask him, "Do you love me?" First, he doesn't know. I remember when I was 15 years old and my wife was then my girlfriend. We have been together since I was 14 and she was 15. We didn't have cell phones back then and our family couldn't afford to have a phone in our house at that time. I was so caught up in my wife that I walked from my house to the public pay phone about a half mile away. To hear her voice, I would have walked farther if I had to. Let me set the stage for you so you get a mental picture of what this looked like. She was in a nice, dry house. I was in the rain on a pay phone to which I had walked. While on the phone, I told her, "I love you." Her response (from her nice, dry house) to me (who was out in the pouring rain) was, "No, you don't." I said, "Yes, I do." She said, "You're infatuated." I'm like, "What? I'm on the phone in the rain and I'm telling you I love you, girl." She said, "You're infatuated." Then she had the nerve to say, "Do you know what that means?" I was like, "No." She said, "Then go home and look it up." She helped me that day!

In actuality, that was the best thing she could have said. Why? Because I didn't know if I loved her. I was saying it but I didn't know what love was at that time. A male man who doesn't understand fatherhood will give you all kinds of reasons why he loves you. He'll say, "Oh, I love you. The sun reflects your glory. I love you. The stars shine bright with your reflection." He'll say, "Listen to that. Do you hear the wind? It's saying, 'I love you,' girl. I love you." He'll say all types of things, trying to tell you he loves you, but that's not the question to ask him. Ask him, "Can you cultivate me?" Ask him, "Can you sustain me?" Ask him, "Can you maintain me? Can you provide for me? Can you protect me? Do you have a prayer life? Where is your prayer life? Have you had a garden experience?" Ask him the right things. Don't ask him about loving you. He doesn't know what love is at that point. He doesn't know if he loves you. And if he says that he does, he is only infatuated and has an ulterior motive.

To the single ladies reading this book, know that we have been cultivating you since page one. We've been tilling your ground spiritually, cultivating it. When ground gets tilled, weeds will grow unless the proper seeds are planted and the soil is cared for. Don't allow all this revelation about fatherhood and the standards that God set for husbands to be undone by allowing some slick-looking weeds to invade your soil. How can you tell if he is a weed? If he's a real man, he will want to meet one of two people: your natural father or your spiritual father. If he's a real man, he will say, "Take me to your father." If he's a real man, before he can establish any relationship with you, he must have a relationship with your father, natural or spiritual. If he doesn't want to meet your father, he's a weed. If you don't have a relationship with your father or your father has gone on to be with the Lord, you have a spiritual father. The first person you should bring him to is fatherhood in your life.

If he approaches you in a manner that is not in alignment with the way in which your father would operate, that should be a telltale sign that he is not ready for you. Why would you leave the Fatherhood of God or the fatherhood of a good natural father to connect with someone who does not live up to their standards? If all he can see are your physical attributes, he is not ready! He is a weed who will choke out any harvest in your life. Bring any suitor to the fatherhood in your life. Let those men check him out. For me, in about five minutes I can tell whether he's the one. I can just look in his eyes. I have had to tell this to some women. It was hard to hear but those women are better because they did not allow a weed to enter their lives. Many men are trained to be weeds. They take nutrients from the well-maintained soil but as they grow, they destroy everything around them. I know about weeds because I used to be one! I believe some of the men reading this book would say the same about themselves. Some have not stopped being a weed. I thank God that I was a weed for only a little while because I can spot it. Once you've been there, you can identify a weed.

Single ladies, you must be able to identify weeds. If you just listen, if you're quiet and let him talk, you can hear the sounds of life being choked out. When we were younger, I told my wife, "If I was your man, girl, you wouldn't want for anything." I was broke and had nothing; I was just "spitting game" to her. All weeds want to do is invade your good soil. Weeds cherish commitment. They want to get in and take over until nothing is left. Weeds sometimes look good from a distance but when you get close to them, you see their destructive nature. They are not good for your precious ground.

God has called for your ground to be continually developed and cultivated, for the right seed to be put there. Single ladies, you must put some type of sign in your ground saying, "No weeds welcome here." You need to spray some spiritual pesticide on your ground to keep the weeds away.

final word

W hat I am about to share with you, men, is something I have intentionally held back as we've taken this journey together. Everything I have shared with you up to this point has been to get you to this place of revelation. Since you've been reading this book, something has been taking place inside you. Buckle your seatbelts, gentlemen, because you're about to take off. The whole time you have been reading this, ten people have been coming alive in you. I am not talking about split personalities but rather the ten men God intentionally put in you from your birth. The same way a seed has multiple trees inside it, God has put ten individuals inside you. There's a source inside you, a sustainer inside you, a protector inside you, a leader inside you, a teacher inside you, a disciplinarian inside you, a progenitor inside you, an upholder inside you, a caretaker inside you and a cultivator inside you.

When the devil comes up against a man who says, "You're not dealing with me; you're dealing with ten in one. You're dealing with ten men on the inside of me who know who they are and who will not back down. You might knock me down but the other nine will pick me back up because I know who I am," satan will think twice about attacking you. He'll deal with one but now, when he looks at ten, he knows he's outnumbered. When he looks at ten fatherhood people inside of one, that's when he tucks his tail and retreats. He does not want to deal with ten men inside of one. He wasn't expecting that. The devil tries to use the hurt from your past to exploit you and defeat you. However, when you have awakened the ten men inside you, he has no hope of defeating you. When you have revelation of who you really are, you transform into ten. You multiply into ten.

You now have ten of you who will rise up, and when they rise up you're dealing with a fortified man. Single daughters, catch this concerning a potential mate; you must see all ten in one. Don't simply see his good looks, his bank account or the type of car he drives. Can you see the ten in him? When you can see the ten, you have a man who not only can take care of himself, but who can be a true husband to you. If you go off just good looks, you have one who's no match for the enemy. Good looks will fade. Muscles will drop. A thin waistline will protrude. It's called *time*. Hair will recede and backslide. That stuff will go, but the ten will stay.

Ladies, even when you don't feel that you're worthy in the natural, the ten in him will stay. Wives, even when you mess up and open the spiritual doors that allow the enemy to walk in, the ten in him will deal with the enemy and shut the spiritual door. The ten men in him will never settle for him sleeping on the couch and not talking to you. The ten men in him will always unite and cause him to put his arms around you even when you're not lovable. The man who truly understands the ten-in-one principle will go to work in the morning and bring himself back home at night. While he's away, there's no worry in your mind about where he is. You know he's not cheating. You know he's not doing anything to dishonor God. You know he's working. He's building up the family. When he's not there, he's still there. When the provider part of him is out working, the source part, sustainer part, and other seven parts of him will still be at home with you because of what he has developed in the family. The kids will be in order and there will not be a tone of "Wait for your daddy to come home" because Daddy's presence is there right now. The leader is there. The teacher is there. Discipline is there. When you have ten in one, the wife and children are covered at all times, in all places.

Ladies, don't look for one; look for ten. If you don't see ten, stay single until the tenth one comes forward. Even if he says, "We've been dating for three years now. Aren't you ready?" "No, because I'm still missing one." "What are you talking about, missing one?" "I don't see the leadership. I don't see the disciplinarian. I don't see the source." "You don't understand. I have a disability so I can't work." "Well, I need to see a man who can sustain."

If you're married and you don't see all ten right now in your husband, you need to speak to God and declare and decree. No negative talk about him, saying, "You're trifling. You need to read this book because you don't measure up." Don't do that. Speak into him. "You're a man of God. There are ten in one in you. I see everything that God has called you to." Call the ten in one into his life. Help him become the ten.

If you're single, don't be swayed by sweet talk. Sweet talk may get you to the altar but it won't keep you in marriage. Even if the person has a number of degrees, they mean absolutely nothing. A man with no degree can still have the ten in one. This book has laid out a standard for determining whether a man is sent from God or sent as a distraction. You're after a man walking with the fatherhood anointing, one who will lead you to church and not the other way around. The key is the ten in one. I'm trying to show you what you should be seeing. As a single woman, if after reading this book you turn around and connect yourself with something other than the ten-in-one man, shame on you.

Every man who has read this book, if you aren't lining up now with what you've heard, it's not the devil; it's you. You need to line up. You have had page after page, chapter after chapter, showing you where you must change or where you must identify things and make the change. You must line up. There's nothing else. There are no excuses. Your background and where you came from don't matter now. You're equipped to turn around and be the father God has called you to be.

As a single man, if you're not all ten, don't you dare get into a relationship. What do you have to offer? Nothing.

As I conclude, I hope you caught the heart of this project. This information is to lead both men and women to a revelation of what God has intended in the earth and what satan has been trying to stop concerning fatherhood. The family is under attack by satan. If he can destroy the family, he can destroy communities and towns and cities and nations. The devil understands that the way he will destroy those things is through the male man. The devil must get the male man out of the picture because the male man is the foundation.

I exhort every man reading this right now, as the foundation of everything in this earth, to rise up and be the ten in one you have been called to be. Regardless of where you have been, it's not too late to line up and head toward where you are supposed to be. Don't quit, don't give up, don't concede and don't wave the white flag. There are ten men in you roaring to get out. I have opened the door for you but only you can let them out. Your family needs you to let them out, the church needs you to let them out and this world needs you to let them out. You are the Missing Link.